Literatures of the Americas

Series Editor
Norma E. Cantú
Trinity University
San Antonio, TX, USA

This series seeks to bring forth contemporary critical interventions within a hemispheric perspective, with an emphasis on perspectives from Latin America. Books in the series highlight work that explores concerns in literature in different cultural contexts across historical and geographical boundaries and also include work on the specific Latina/o realities in the United States. Designed to explore key questions confronting contemporary issues of literary and cultural import, *Literatures of the Americas* is rooted in traditional approaches to literary criticism but seeks to include cutting-edge scholarship using theories from postcolonial, critical race, and ecofeminist approaches.

More information about this series at
http://www.palgrave.com/gp/series/14819

Ricardo L. Ortiz

Latinx Literature Now

Between Evanescence and Event

Ricardo L. Ortiz
Department of English
Georgetown University
Georgetown, DC, USA

Literatures of the Americas
ISBN 978-3-030-04707-8   ISBN 978-3-030-04708-5   (eBook)
https://doi.org/10.1007/978-3-030-04708-5

Library of Congress Control Number: 2018964584

This Palgrave Macmillan imprint is published by the registered company Springer Nature Switzerland AG
The registered company address is: Gewerbestrasse 11, 6330 Cham, Switzerland

This book, like everything else about my life, is dedicated to the memory of my parents and of my brother José Esteban Muñoz, and to the proofs of hope, and resiliency, and love, I need, and get, every day from my sisters and my nephews.

ACKNOWLEDGEMENTS

This book exists thanks to the intellectual generosity and support of an array of colleagues, mostly at Georgetown University and in the fields of study I call home, who either heard or read and responded to sections of the work as it evolved from as far back as 2007 to the present moment. These include folks who attended sessions at conferences of the American Comparative Literature Association, the American Studies Association, the Modern Language Association, the Latino Studies Association, the Cuban Research Institute where I shared work, as well as "works-in-progress" groups closer to home, like the Americas Initiative of Georgetown College and the Georgetown English Department's "First Monday" lunch series. It also exists thanks to support in the form of a series of Summer Academic Grants awarded either by Georgetown University's Faculty Research Council or by the Georgetown English Department.

Beyond parties who were directly supportive of the work contained here, there are also numerous other professional networks which have welcomed me over the years and sustained me intellectually, emotionally, and personally in larger ways that also contributed to making this book possible. These include my colleagues and students at Georgetown in the Departments of English, History, and Performing Arts, the Programs in American Studies, Comparative Literature, and Justice and Peace Studies, the Centers for Latin American Studies, Multicultural Equity and Access, New Designs in Learning and Scholarship, and Social Justice Research, Teaching, and Service, and the Offices of the President, the Provost, the Dean of Georgetown College, and Mission and Ministry. Beyond Georgetown, I have counted myself lucky to belong to the DC-area Queer Studies Reading Group, the national MLA-led and Mellon-funded Connected Academics project, and the community of colleagues centrally involved in the work of the Latino Studies Association, especially those directly responsible for organizing the 2018 LSA conference in Washington, DC.

The following people I name by name because of the miraculous and joyful ways that colleagues can become friends can become family: Elizabeth Vélez, Antonio López, Randall Cole, Leona Fisher, Sherry Linkon, Maureen Corrigan, Carolyn Forché, Kathryn Temple, Randall Bass, Derek Goldman, John Tutino, Verónica Salles-Reese, Gwen Kirkpatrick, Nancy Raquel Mirabal, Lázaro Lima, John Morán González, Robert Kaner, Jocelyn Medawar, Samantha Pinto, Charlene Brown-McKenzie, Shiva Subbaraman, Dennis Williams, Eddie Maloney, Matthew Tinkcom, Christine So, Patrick O'Malley, Paul O'Neill, Jaime Briseño, David Olsen, David Román, William Atkins, Jennifer Doyle, Carla Marcantonio, Karen Jaime, Raquel Gutiérrez, Israel Reyes, Esteban García, Angie Bonilla, and Joshua Javier Guzmán.

PRAISE FOR *LATINX LITERATURE NOW*

"I read Ricardo Ortiz's *Latinx Literature Now* and fell in love. Writing with grace and uncanny theoretical wisdom, Ortiz deftly demonstrates we are at a new moment in Latinx literary studies, one that finds scholars wrestling with the relationship between the epistemological claims of literature, theory and history and the ontological dimensions of what we call Latinx literature. The evanescence and event of this literature bubbles up in the unique pairings and stunning interpretations Ortiz offers—Jacques Derrida and Edwidge Danticat; Julia Alvarez and Hayden White; John Beverly, Rigoberta Menchú, and Reinaldo Arenas, among others. A first-rate intellectual achievement!"
—Ralph E. Rodriguez, *author of* Latinx Literature Unbound *and*
Brown Gumshoes

"Ricardo Ortiz's concise and rich study is a *tour de force* that incisively explains the unfolding of contemporary US Latinx literature. Latinx writing itself becomes a historical act capable of making valid and productive claims to knowledge and truth. Incisive and theoretically capacious, this bold book offers a timely analysis that is necessary reading for anyone wanting to understand what Latinx literature does."
—Rafael Pérez-Torres, *UCLA, US*

"Don't let the brevity of this project fool you. This *tour de force* is an extended rumination that unfolds beautifully and provocatively through a number of untried questions that have too long been dormant in Latinx literary studies. In characteristic fashion—and in ways that mirror the very arguments he makes for the way we might approach/read/collaborate/activate the afterlives of Latinx literary texts themselves—Ortiz treats his reader with generosity, inviting us to participate in this unfolding with him, to think deeply and slowly and in new ways about the relationship between history and literature, between diaspora and nation, between Latinx, Hispaniolan, and Caribbean literature."

—Sandra K. Soto, *University of Arizona, USA*

CONTENTS

INTRODUCTION

This essay offers itself as an opportunity to reflect on, and to make some claims concerning, a set of expressive cultural practices, primarily organized around whatever might qualify them as acts of Latinx literature, and a set of critical and scholarly practices, especially those which, like literary studies, cultural studies, history, American studies, Latin American studies and US Latinx studies, might avow a set of discipline- and field-specific interests in accounting for how some rough concatenation of US Latinx literary production, and a corresponding concatenation of US Latinx literary studies, might be said to have done (and to continue to be doing) whatever work defines them in their respective spaces and modes of practice, and how that work in turn self-collates, not only into a process, or a practice, or even a *project*, but as something ineluctably either still-just happening, or not-yet happening, or about-to happen, but always in some still-current state of immanent emergence and evanescence that allows us to find ourselves (still!) just-hailing the event we will have come to have known to have been "US Latinx Literature."[1] This discussion will in its long course turn to work in both the philosophy of literature and the philosophy of history to articulate more clearly how such claims about an object or event we could call "literature" can only come from the para-practical space outside of literature itself,[2] that even when a literary text avows itself *as* literature, it can only do so by miming extra-literary discourses, like history or philosophy or criticism or theory, in order to enact that self-naming, that claim to self-knowledge.[3] As it moves forward, this discussion will try to fashion a sense of the event that alternates between the persistence of its ineluctability and its equally persistent evanescence, where the very appearance of a formation like US *latinidad* (not to mention US Latinx *literature*) only ever makes itself available through the threat or the risk of its vanishing, of its immediate re/dis/appearance, back into marginalization, oblivion, and silence. This sense of the evanescent "event-ness" of US Latinx/literature will, therefore, refuse to decide between its (their) potential momentousness and its (their) equally potential momentariness. And while this essay leans heavily in the direction of a plausible construction of *latinidad* as itinerant, evanescent and precarious (thus suggesting an emphasis on aspects of it tied closely to direct experiences of immigration, non-documentation, non-enfranchisement, and extreme necro-/bio-/political vulnerability), it does not at all mean to imply that such a construction should absolutely trump existing and well-established accounts of more stably nationalist and historic constructions, some of them extending back to the early nineteenth and covering all of the twentieth century, of Chican@/x, mainland Puerto Rican, Cuban-American, Dominican-American, etc., identity and community emanating from those various (sub-)fields.[4]

Since the question of the status of *literature* will take up the bulk of this essay's work, the related question for us of the status of *latinidad* will take up some detailed attention in the following section, if only to clear some fertile historical and conceptual ground, to introduce the work of two scholars who will both explicitly and implicitly inform the rest of this discussion, and to take some early steps in the process of bringing our two key terms into active, productive dialectical engagement. The rest of the succeeding sections below can be read as a series of congruent but also independent attempts to describe the behaviors of Latinx literary textuality, as simultaneously historical processes of production and reception, and across a collection of writers, texts, and theories that all lay compelling claims to touchstone status in the work of Latinx literary practice, and Latinx literary criticism, as the second decade of the twenty-first century turns toward the third. For reasons that the following sections make clear, this project draws more from Latin American rather than US Latinx literary studies scholarship, but it also draws amply from both, and along the way it engages work by a variety of mostly non-Latinx figures (including Sigmund Freud, Jacques Derrida, Hayden White, and Michel-Rolphe Trouillot) from critical theory that touches language, literature, and history, as well as tracing a genealogy of literary texts, mostly produced in the quarter century following nineteen ninety-two, the fifth centennial of the New World's collision with the Columbus expedition, and proceeding from work produced by writers in the larger US Caribbean diaspora to work originating in Central American and Chicanx America. Readers will also note a set of strategic pairings along the way, from John Beverley with Cristina Beltrán, to Edwidge Danticat with Jacques Derrida, to Reinaldo Arenas with Rigoberta Menchú, pairings that hopefully trouble productively the logics of genre, discourse, and discipline along the way, troubling the conventions of those logics of categorization enough to allow us to read, and to know, US Latinx literature differently than we have yet historically, and perhaps therefore, actually, to see it for the first time.

NOTES

1. This essay takes its cues for its own characterization of a mostly potentialized construction of *latinidad* from José Esteban Muñoz's analogous construction of queerness as future utopian projection and wish in *Cruising Utopia: The There and Then of Queer Futurity* (New York University Press, 2009). For this reason, it understands *latinidad*'s own current and ongoing potentialization as all promise and no guarantees; rather than serving as an ontological or epistemological ground for the basis of any claim, therefore, we will only project a *latinidad* as desire, as wish, and as *project*: that is, as a not-yet-realized occasion for the production of resources for survival and cultivation, resources to be shared, and enjoyed, in (what José had begun to call a brown) common(s). This essay, and any related future work from its writer, is dedicated to José's memory, and to a deep hope for all the possible afterlives of his work.

2. In the last section we will lean toward Terry Eagleton's characterization of the ontological performativity of the literary act and/or literary event (in 2010's *The Event of Literature*, Yale University Press), which explicitly reaches back as far as Austin's work in *How to Do Things with Words* (Harvard University Press, 1962) and at least implicitly runs through rather than around Jacques Derrida's deconstructive engagement with speech-act-school performativity in and out of literary contexts, from 1972's "Signature, Event, Context" in *Limited Inc* (trans. Samuel Weber, Northwestern University Press, 1988), through his 1991 collaboration with Derek Attridge on the collection *Acts of Literature* (Routledge, 1992). It will also trace aspects of Judith Butler's primarily post-structural, de-ontological critique of gender identity/subjectivity as performative, especially as it influences related work, like Cristina Beltrán's strategic

re-eventuation of a political US Latin@ identity as itself analogously performative. It will, however, and mostly due to restrictions of space, only briefly glance at the recent post-post-structural "return" of a philosophical ontology in work like Alain Badiou's. At best here we can cite other scholars who, like John Beverley in *Latinamericanism After 9/11*, mention Badiou for their own purposes (7). But I suspect that some threads within Latinx studies, like Lázaro Lima's characterization in *The Latino Body* (2007) of the "becoming-historical" of a visible, legible, effective Latinx subjectivity in the US American context, have been anticipating this return to ontology before Badiou's work became better known in the Anglophone world; and, in fact, applications of Badiou's work in corresponding fields (like James Tweedie's work in film studies: "The Event of Cinema," *Cultural Critique*, Fall 2012) also suggest ways in which he may have positive contributions to make across all fields beholden in part to politically engaged post-structural cultural studies methodologies.

3. See, for example, how both the passage from Junot Díaz discussed in our last section, and a text as literary-historical as Julia Alvarez's novel *In the Name of Salomé* (also discussed in detail below) both operate simultaneously as acts of literary, literary-historical, and literary-critical, practice.

4. Work certainly remains to be done on the various intellectual, institutional and ideological rationales for how any and all of these various fields should interact and inter-implicate one another.

CHAPTER 1

The Trouble(s) with Unity: Performative Latinidades Between Culture and Politics

Abstract Using work published over the first decade of the twenty-first century by scholars John Beverley and Cristina Beltrán, "The Trouble(s) with Unity" opens the larger discussion by accounting for US *latinidad* as a demographic, historical, political, and cultural formation, one better characterized by fluidity, heterogeneity, unevenness, and nonidentity than by any more conventional, categorical, essentialist or in any other way fixed identitarian logics.

Keywords *Latinidad* · Latinx · Latinamericanism · Identity · Performativity · Politics

Late in the "Introduction" to his 2004 collection, *Testimonio: On the Politics of Truth*, the Latin Americanist cultural studies scholar John Beverley refers briefly but pointedly to one then-underreported facet of the September 11, 2001 terrorist attacks on the United States. While those attacks, he observes, were "directed against a homogeneous corporate-imperial America, symbolized by the Pentagon and the World Trade Center, [their] immediate aftermath revealed instead a 'real' multicultural, middle- and working-class America among the victims" (24–25).[1] Beverley remembers the revelation of the "multicultural" cast to that population of victims, especially among people working that day in the twin towers in lower Manhattan, as occurring repeatedly in ritual performance in the intervening years: "In the symbolic readings of the names of the dead on the anniversary of September 11," he recalls, "—a common form of testimonial commemoration—a significant number were Hispanic. Many of them, we know, were illegal immigrants from countries like El Salvador and Guatemala, fleeing ... counterrevolutionary violence, ... and working for minimum wage in the interstices of the new global cities" (25). I wrote a very early draft of this essay in September of 2014, using Beverley's then-decade-old reference to an even more distant but still insistent act of mass atrocity, whose actual victims included perhaps surprisingly large numbers of undocumented workers from Central America, to underscore the political and historical distance traveled, or not traveled, between 2004 and 2014, a distance even more appallingly vast from the vantage of 2018. That summer of 2014 saw, as one of a number of troubling instances of excessive state aggression colliding with either catastrophic state failure or increasingly violent (and mostly criminal) political action on the part of non-state entities against actual (often certainly not entirely innocent) states,[2] reports of an unprecedented humanitarian immigrant crisis on the southern border of the United States, a crisis involving many tens of thousands of unaccompanied and undocumented minors from some of the same countries in Central America mentioned in John Beverley's 2004 piece referring to 2001. Readers familiar with the exacerbation of these already fraught dynamics, occasioned first by the election to the US Presidency of Donald J. Trump in November of 2016, and afterwards by the long series of Trump Administration anti-immigrant policies that led by the summer of 2018 to the crisis surrounding immigrant families separated at the US southern border, will understand how a historical process already decades underway in 2011 continue to unfold in their devastating relentlessness against the very same vulnerable populations from the same nations and communities.

In that 2004 chapter, Beverley labels that population of murdered undocumented immigrants as already "Hispanic," and I want to pause at this act of demographic categorization and ethnic naming to initiate my own reflections on the precariousness and instability of both "Hispanic," Beverley's term of use and also *Latinx*,[3] the primary alternative to "Hispanic" that other critics and scholars might employ in reference to roughly the same group today. Beverley's rhetorical construction of the "Latinx" dimension of 9/11 underscores for me something of the ongoing challenge (even in 2018) to any US Latinx studies *practice*, and certainly to anything that might want to claim to work as a US Latinx

political *project*, given what we might term the persistent and even recalcitrant historical (perhaps, indeed, ontological) evanescence of some part
of the demographic object-in-question that these projects might want
to name as demonstrably, substantially, and coherently "*Latinx.*" What
possible historical, political and cultural status, we might ask, accrues
to the multitude of bodies of murdered persons who found themselves
living and working without legal documentation in a geographical zone
that pulls them simultaneously toward a past that explains their precarious situation in the present moment of their collective murder (that is,
toward the historical space dominated by the narrative protagonism of
the nation-state, where they can be said to have fled countries ravaged
by "[counter-]revolutionary violence" fueled in large part by the foreign
policy of the imperial state where they later find themselves working,
living, and dying, without papers) and toward a future they themselves
will not survive to see (but one where the historical-narrative monop-
oly of the nation-state begins to recede in favor of trans-national, supra-
national, and sub-national formations that will tend increasingly toward
the non- and even anti-national, located here in Beverley's reference to
"the interstices of the new global cities"). In the years following 2001,
one could already experience a kind of conceptual vertigo in attempting
to account, historically, for how this "undocumented" population with
no official sanction to work or to live in the nation-state they inhabited
and labored to serve, and clean, and build, would still find commemoration as nameable, hence to that extent legitimate(d) and meaningful victims (or even martyrs?) *for* that nation-state, so much so that their names
could be read aloud at public, sanctioned events commemorating their
deaths, their martyrdoms, at Ground Zero and elsewhere, everywhere
that such commemorations were (and still continue to be) held.

Yet now, in this 2018 of the post-Obama Trump era, a corresponding conceptual vertigo might set in if we consider in turn: many of the
children and older adolescents attempting to reach US American ground
in and since the summer of 2014, including those migrating with their
parents, were attempting to reach relatives, including parents, who were
already in the United States, with or without papers of their own; many
of these relatives had already lived and worked in the United States for
years, and had already had US-born children or otherwise formed deep
affective and practical ties with family and communities in the United
States; and finally, most of the young people traveling north did so to
escape persecution, physical and sexual assault and possible murder, at

the hands of mostly drug-running urban gangs which, like MS-13 and
the 18th Street gang, have their origins in US American cities like Los
Angeles and Washington, DC.[4] Regardless of how little direct experience
most of these young immigrants had had of the United States before
arriving into its national territorial space, how is their experience not
always-already a "US Latinx" formation?[5] Certainly while these unaccompanied and separated children, bereft of both parental protection
and the formal legal protection of state documentation, present their
own unique version of a kind of biopolitical precarity, it doesn't quite
match that accrued by the Latinx "martyrs," whose own precarity saw
eventual, if ironic, redemption according to the logic of a prevailing
post-9/11 US American national symbolic of mourning.[6] Both episodes,
however, together tell us something about how one ongoing formation
unfolding in the current historical moment, one that emphatically takes
on the designation of "US Latinx," in doing so also reveals a great deal
about the increasing precarity of the national state form itself, certainly
for smaller, more vulnerable states that continue barely to survive violent
transnational forces (from the Cold War, to the drug wars, to a resur-
gent "war on terror," to all the various pressures and demands of the
global neoliberal political economy), but also for larger, even imperial
and hegemonic, national states experiencing the gradual but persistent
withering away of their historical dominance.[7]

By the time he publishes *Latinamericanism After 9/11* (his follow-
up to the 2004 *Testimonio* collection) in 2011, John Beverley can make
the following bracing declaration: "The reality on the ground," as a
general condition of political life in the Americas of the early twenty-
first century, "is that the border is an increasingly anachronistic and
violent fiction" (2011, 16). To the extent that such a *fiction*, especially
in all the ways that such a diagnosis applies to the general movement of
Latin Americans to the United States, can explain the northern imperial
hegemon's increasing encounter with its own internal racial, ethnic and
cultural complexity and otherness to itself, it stages a scene in the 2011
"Introduction" that neatly corresponds in practice to the one posed in
theory in 2004. If, in theory, an adequately "radical multiculturalism"
can "propose to redefine the identity of both the nation and the international order, ... ask[ing] of the state not 'recognition' of [its, multiculturalism's] alterity, but rather that the state recognize itself as other:
that it is always-already multicultural," (2004, 24), then, in practice,

even the mere "demographic" pressure of an "exploding" Latinx population might "oblige ... the United States [to] become as a nation something other than it is (or imagines itself to be) today" (2011, 16). By
2011, of course, some aspects of the looming Latinx challenge to the
US American national cultural imaginary that Beverley could antic-
ipate in 2004 had already started to materialize: one can point briefly,
at least at the level of national politics, to the extraordinary protests in
favor of immigration reform across the United States in 2006, to the rising influence of US Latinx voters in the national elections of 2008 (and
again later in 2012), and to the on-again-off-again national prominence
of debates and activism surrounding the DREAM Act, the Obama-era
DACA and DAPA policies, and more comprehensive attempts at immigration reform since at least 2006 and across the ongoing US American
Trump era (even ignoring here both positive political developments at
the state, local and regional levels, as well as the more negative, harm-
ful and desperate attempts of primarily conservative, nativist political
forces to tighten by further militarizing border security, and intensifying
law enforcement and deportation practices against undocumented persons already settled and committed to building their US American lives).
Underlying much of this movement at social, political and historical levels is the irresistible force of unprecedented demographic growth: "[W]
ith a Hispanic population currently estimated at forty five million and
rapidly growing," Beverley could write in 2011, "the United States is
on the road to becoming in the next ten years or so, after Mexico, the
second-largest nation of the Spanish-speaking world, surpassing Spain
itself in that regard" (15); for this reason Beverley can conclude later in
the essay, and in a phrase that echoes his prediction of 2004, that "the
United States will have to become as a nation something other than it is
(or imagines itself to be) today" (16).[8]

    In roughly the same historical moment that John Beverley was tracing
the shifting contours and proposing the compelling promise of a decidedly post-9/11, and compellingly trans-hemispheric critical Latin(x)
americanism, the US-based political scientist and theorist Cristina
Beltrán was producing one of the more sustained, comprehensive, and
theoretically rigorous analyses of the specifically US-based formation of
latinidad to appear by that point, in her 2010 study, *The Trouble with
Unity: Latino Politics and the Creation of Identity*. Beltrán's more capacious conceptual work in that volume will frame for us our own more

specific considerations of US Latinx *literary* studies' ongoing attempts, even as 2018 turns toward 2019 and beyond, to come to coherent and productive critical terms with its own shifting primary object of study, an object still undergoing complex alchemical mutations thanks to the ongoingly stubborn undecidabilities of its two constituent elements, *literature* and *latinidad*. Not surprisingly, Beltrán at times takes recourse to the same terminology of ineluctable ontology that Beverley used to describe the ongoing Latinization of US American society in the decade following 11 September 2001. Beltrán opens her discussion by referring to a much older and longer-lived Latinx formation, the more than 30-year old pattern in US American public discourse of describing the looming but not-yet-realized impact of the growing US Latinx population on US American political life in terms of a "sleeping giant, … a symbol of presence, a figure whose size makes it impossible to ignore and whose growing influence will surely impact every aspect of American cultural and political life" (5). Beltrán will take effective issue with both implications of this looming (if still somnolent) but significantly forceful "presence," questioning simultaneously the presumably consensual unicity implicit in the singular formation of that Latinx "presence" (which, she'll argue, "is not one") and the "causal" logic of historical potentiality and eventuality that insists on casting political *latinidad* in the United States *as* (still) a unified "cause," one that has yet to achieve its most logically compelling effect, whatever that one thing, that one event, might (yet) turn out to be.

Beltrán quickly dispenses with this still-prevailing locution as she opens her study, insisting from her opening on that US-based *latinidad* has been for decades if not any longer an ongoing process, one both riven and driven by heterogeneity, complexity, dissension, and discontinuity. While "*Latinidad,*" Beltrán argues, chiefly names "the sociohistorical process whereby various Latin American national-origin groups are understood as sharing a sense of collective identity and cultural consciousness" (4), the actual "*process* of Latinidad is both complex and contradictory, involving issues of immigration, colonialism, conquest, race, color, gender, sexuality, class and language" (5) and therefore belies any suggestion of especially but not only political unity and consensus in any invocation of a "pan-ethnic Leviathan" (6). Beltrán's insistence here in moving from a construction of *latinidad* as static, essential, and essentialist, entity to something that can take further steps toward activism and agency by moving from historical process to something that might begin to look like political practice obliges her, however, to export some conceptual resources and theoretical strategies from disciplines other than political science. *The Trouble with Unity*, she tells us, "takes a ... post-structural approach" to its topic, "recognizing Latino identity as always historically and discursively constructed," and following in part Judith Butler's decades of work on the performativity of gender to argue that an ethnic construction like "Latino' ... should be reconceived as a site of permanent political contestation ... of ongoing resignifiability—as a political rather than descriptive category" (9).[9] Clearly her references to post-structuralism, discursive construction, gender performativity, and (re-)signifiability signal to her readers that she's in very direct conversation with critical humanities work interested in the politics of ethnicity and identity, and as that work has already seen active productivity in "the fields of English, cultural and American studies, anthropology, comparative literature, media studies and performance studies" (13). Beltrán closes her introduction to *The Trouble with Unity* by insisting that, instead of positively calling for or celebrating some form of political disunity or dissolution of the US Latinx political project, what she offers is a productive, even practical deconstruction of a category that really could never withstand sustained critical and analytical pressure.

What she offers instead, Beltrán tells us, is an "explicitly political understanding of Latino identity, in which political subjectivity is recognized as inescapably fragmented and where agonistic identities are foundational to its democratic project" (19). As we observed earlier, Beltrán arrives at this newly "political" construction of *latinidad* via her engagement with Judith Butler's political theorization of the irreducible performativity of gender to make a corresponding case for the effective performativity of a politicized *latinidad*. Beltrán thus encourages us to see "*Latinidad* as action—as something we do rather than something we are ... as an assertion rather than an answer ... as a site of ongoing resignifiability–as protean, yet not unrecognizable" (19). The present discussion will bracket the explicitly political repercussions that Beltrán posits as issuing from her conceptual intervention in order to emphasize, as I do above, her acknowledged debts to culture-based critical theory, and especially to a discursive, expressive performativity, one that leans significantly in the direction of even *literary* practice, and that in important ways models how a move away from the static (identitarian) essentialism (which almost always resorts to violent, exclusionary forms of forced consensus) that might have characterized older forms of identity politics allows the fuller consideration of actual political ontologies grounded in discernible, and dirigible, process and practice. This, then, is the moment when the present discussion can take its own pivotal turn, from the long consideration of *latinidad* as practice just undertaken, to an imbricating consideration of *literature*, as itself a practice and a project, always-already haunting whatever life, and whatever hope, *latinidad* has ever even able to claim, or to pursue.[10]

We can therefore hit pause here on this discussion of the ways that a US-based *latinidad* continues into 2018 to emerge as a shifting, heterogeneous, and evanescent formation, and thank John Beverley and Cristina Beltrán for providing us with rich, complex, and useful analyses of that formation from the larger hemispheric and critical perspectives that Latin American and US Latinx cultural studies can provide. We'll return in later sections to some of Beverley's more explicitly literary-critical work. At this point, however, it bears making one important complicating corrective to Beverley's account of the ongoing "Latin(x)" Americanization of the United States: that it has not been nor will it be exclusively a "Spanish-speaking," hispanophone formation (something Beltrán at least implies in her work as well). We'll turn now, as we pivot from *latinidad* (back) to *literature* (and without actually leaving *latinidad* behind), and toward a literary-critical genealogy which issues from French, francophone, and Caribbean-Haitian kreyòl sources, and which we can signify at least once here as a corollary formation of *latinité*. That genealogy directly informs the analysis that takes up the following section, involving a (hopefully) productive encounter between one of the seminal texts of post-structural deconstruction, Jacques Derrida's 1972 essay "Signature, Event, Context," and a more recent manifesto of a generally contemporary "immigrant" literary practice, Edwidge Danicat's 2010 essay "Create Dangerously: The Immigrant Artist at Work."[11]

NOTES

1. My analysis of the current construction(s) of US Latinx identity relies implicitly on work like Lázaro Lima's in *The Latino Body* (2007), where he theorizes US Latinidad as a "crisis identity." "Crisis identities," according to Lima, "are ... always grounded in the recognition of a capitulation that seeks an explanation or resolution in and though narrative ... [;] the term signals a philosophical inquiry into the structures of consciousness experienced from what could be understood as the narrative first-person point of view, the *cogito* before the *ergo sum*" (6). Analyses like Lima's of identity as itself always potentially a crisis-formation receive transformative elaboration in Robin Wiegman's work throughout *Object Lessons* (2012), where she critically surveys many of the various post-1960s fields of "identity studies" claiming to produce "identity knowledges" in both the United States and international university contexts. In a long roster of its possible "registers" within or as which identity conceptually, categorically and strategically works, Wiegman lists the following: "a coordinate of power, social formation, mode of interpellation, discourse of state and self-designation, political horizon, interpretative practice, field of study, or institutional emblem of difference" (8). To this menu of options for the operation of *latinidad* specifically, it's likely that most practitioners in the field of US Latinx studies might agree to answer, "yes, all of the above," even as we observe that the list actually excludes vital additional "registers" of intimacy, domesticity, community, desire, affect and even spirituality where we might claim either to experience directly or at least to encounter and recognize (our) *latinidad*.
2. The litany of news media titular shorthands will have to suffice here: ISIS in Syria and Iraq and beyond; Israel, Palestine, Gaza; Ferguson, Baltimore, St. Louis, Standing Rock; eastern Ukraine, Catalunya, Kurdistan; Brexit and Putin and Duterte and Trump.
3. What I will not do here is engage in the by-now decades-old debate concerning the competing connotations and mostly political efficacies of "Hispanic" versus "Latino, Latina, Latina/o, Latino@, Latinx"; to my mind that debate has been settled in favor of "Latinx" in the scholarly and critical circles within which I run. In addition, I myself employ the notation "Latinx" (rather than Latin[-o/a], [-a/o], or the even clunkier "Latino and Latina" or the outdatedly binaristic "Latin@"), exploiting the negating gesture of the "x" to refuse the gendering of substantives and modifiers in Spanish, knowing that doing so pulls the signifier away from the zone of Hispanophone orthographic correctness but also not necessarily toward any recognizable Anglophone formation, and also away from any familiar oral/aural pronunciation, in any given language.

I will however, resort to those alternative inscriptions of "Latinx" when writers I quote resort to them first. While I have been strategically selective in my decision to focus so exclusively on Beverley and Beltrán for my own elaboration of *latinidad*, my work is also in emphatic if implicit conversation with a genealogy of relevant projects dating back as far as Suzanne Oboler's *Ethnic Labels, Latino Lives: Identity and the Politics of (Re)Presentation in the United States* (University of Minnesota Press, 1995), and including Richard Rodríguez's *Brown: The Last Discovery of America* (Viking, 2002); Juana María Rodriguez's *Queer Latinidad: Identity Practices, Discursive Spaces* (New York UP, 2003); Lázaro Lima's *The Latino Body: Crisis Identities in American Literary and Cultural Memory* (New York UP, 2007); Antonio Viego's *Dead Subjects: Toward a Politics of Loss in Latino Studies* (Duke UP, 2007); Marta Caminero-Santangelo's *On Latinidad: US Latino Literature and the Construction of Ethnicity* (University of Florida Press, 2009); and Claudia Milián's *Latining America: Black-Brown Passages and the Coloring of Latina/o Studies* (Georgia UP, 2013) as well as the contributions of editors and writers to the always-growing number of scholarly collections in the US Latinx studies field and all the various (inter-)disciplines relevant to the field. See also the special issue entitled *Theorizing LatinX* of the journal *Cultural Dynamics* 29: 3 (August 2017) edited and with an introduction by Claudia Milián and featuring pieces by among others Nicole M. Guidotti-Hernández, Antonio Viego, Richard T. Rodríguez, and María de Guzmán; also, the theme of the summer 2018 Latino Studies Association Biennial Conference in Washington, DC, is "Latinx Studies Now."

4. Conditions surrounding the immigration crisis of 2014 were so extreme that they quite directly challenged even the most basic of axioms of modern secular political thought. A June 2014 piece on theatlantic.com even concludes by reporting that young asylum seekers often only succeed in their efforts if they can prove that their persecution by gangs held some kind of political meaning: "In some instances," Julie Turkewitz reports, "winning involves proving to a judge that *a gang has taken on state-like power, making resistance a political act.* 'We have won cases,' said [one attorney]. 'Despite the bad case law'." http://www.theatlantic.com/international/archive/2014/06/credible-fear-whats-driving-central-americans-across-the-us-border/373158/; last accessed on 9 July 2018, emphasis mine.

5. The arc of the narrative of the summer 2014 child immigrant crisis persisted through the fall of that year, although by October it was dramatically eclipsed by all the other major world stories emerging over the same months. Readers can trace the arc of the immigrant story across

this (by no means comprehensive or representative) sample of pieces from the mainstream English langauge press: from 16 June on bbc.com (http://www.bbc.com/news/blogs-echochambers-27874901), to the atlantic.com piece discussed in the previous footnote, to Sonia Nazario's important 11 July piece in *The New York Times* (http://www.nytimes.com/2014/07/13/opinion/sunday/a-refugee-crisis-not-an-immi-gration-crisis.html) to this detailed 30 August *Washington Post* report on what happens to detainees returned to Guatemala (http://www.washingtonpost.com/politics/ellis-island-in-reverse-where-deportees-go-when-they-get-home-to-guatemala/2014/08/28/7b1b0922-2d2b-11e4-9b98-848790384093_story.html). Four years and a radical shift in the implementation of US immigration policy later, conditions of crisis on the US–Mexico border have been severely exacerbated, and the cover-age of them by the national press has duly proliferated, as has the public response.

6. This discussion also owes a mostly implicit debt to Judith Butler's work since roughly 2001 on politics, performativity and "livable" life in mostly "post 9/11" contexts. These projects include: *The Psychic Life of Power: Theories in Subjection* (Stanford UP, 1997); *Precarious Life: The Powers of Mourning and Violence* (Verso, 2004); *Who Sings the Nation-State?: Language, Politics, Belonging* (with Gayatri Spivak, Seagull Books, 2007); and *Frames of War: When Is Life Grievable?* (Verso, 2009).

7. This would be the place for a discussion of the legislative precarity of both the DREAM Act and the DACA/DAPA programs as the Trump presi-dency entrenches itself into its second year.

8. Readers hoping to monitor relevant shifts in the demographic data should consult the website of the Pew Research Hispanic Trends Project: http://www.pewhispanic.org/.

9. For a complementary and foundational project in critical legal race stud-ies, see also Ian F. Haney-López, *White by Law: The Legal Construction of Race* (New York UP, 1996).

10. Briefly, Beltrán concludes the following: "In this vision of politics, energy is directed at building majorities based on shared political visions of social justice rather than the solace (but ultimate frustration) of equating politi-cal agreement with identity" (19).

11. The present essay is the fourth in a series of pieces by its writer to make an explicit case for a broader definition of US *latinidad* that will include a more diverse collection of subjects, especially work by Haitian-American artists like Wyclef Jean and Edwidge Danticat. See in addition: "On (Our-) American Ground: Caribbean-Latino-Diasporic Cultural Production and the Post-National 'Guantanamera'," in *Social Text* 94

(Spring 2008), 3–28; "Edwidge Danticat's *Latinidad: The Farming of Bones* and the Cultivation of (Fields of) Knowledge" in *Aftermaths: Exile, Migration, and Diaspora Reconsidered*, eds. Marcus Bullock and Peter Paik, New Brunswick, NJ, and London: Rutgers UP, 2008; and "Writing the Haitian Diaspora: The Trans-National Contexts of Edwidge Danticat's *The Dew Breaker*," in *Imagined Transnationalism: US Latino/a Literature, Culture and Identity*, eds. Kevin Concannon, Francisco A. Lomelí, and Marc Priewe, New York: Palgrave, 2010: 237–256.

CHAPTER 2

Reiterating Performatives: The Writer, the Reader and the Risks of Literary Action

Abstract "Reiterating Performatives" turns to theoretical work by Jacques Derrida and critical work by Edwidge Danticat to fashion a more capacious, inclusive theory of the writer, and of writing, than those usually understood to have been offered historically by either traditional literary criticism or the strains of post-structural theory that have put that criticism under such acute interrogation over the past fifty years. Without losing sight of the question of latinidad introduced in the previous section, this section focuses primarily on the question of the literary through its analysis of the figure and the work of the writer.

Keywords Writing · Literature · The writer · The author · Precarity · Risk · Evanescence · Deconstruction

Edwidge Danticat, the Haitian-American memoirist, essayist, and fiction writer, opens the first essay of her 2010 collection *Create Dangerously* with the scene of a public political execution in "Papa Doc" François Duvalier's Haiti on 12 November 1964.[1] On that day in Port-au-Prince, two young national liberation activists with the anti-Duvalier Jeune Haiti movement were shot by firing squad in front of a large crowd in the capital's national cemetery; most of those gathered were there under coercion, since Duvalier forced government offices, schools, and other

© The Author(s) 2019
R. L. Ortiz, *Latinx Literature Now*, Literatures of the Americas,
https://doi.org/10.1007/978-3-030-04708-5_2

public offices to close so that a sizeable multitude could witness the act. Danticat uses this occasion as a touchstone for the rest of her meditation in "Create Dangerously," confessing in the opening paragraphs that the event has served her for years as one of the creation narratives of her own coming into being as a writer, both because she owns film footage of the execution (which allows her to describe it in great detail to her reader), and because she shares strong biographical commonalities with the murdered men, who both had gone into exile in the United States when Duvalier *padre* took power, and who both were known to be promising, talented writers. Danticat then goes on to inform us that, in the Port-au-Prince of 1964, one of the ways that young Haitians who opposed Duvalier's dictatorial rule could exercise some limited freedom of expression was through the formation of literary and theatrical clubs that could sponsor readings and performances of expressive, creative work, mostly French, that could put absolutist forms of political power into at least indirect critical scrutiny.

One such association, Danticat tells us, "was called the Club de Bonne Humeur, or the Good Humor Club," which at the time was "reading [Albert] Camus' play *Caligula* with an eye to possibly staging it." Camus composed *Caligula* in the late 1930s and early 1940s, another moment when violent totalitarian power was threatening to engulf the world. Danticat's anecdote about the circulation of Camus' play some decades following its composition, and in a context where the alleviation of the global threat of violent totalitarian oppression continued to meet the persistent and general guarantee of its local occurrence, tells us something useful about the continuing and unfolding dialectic of freedom and power as it plays out in the cultural (and even the literary) field. Camus, Danticat tells us, had serious and understandable reservations about what a play like his could do in the face of the present and looming threat of global fascism; in the preface to an English translation of the play, he confesses: "I look in vain for philosophy in these four acts ... I have little regard for an art that deliberately aims to shock because it is unable to convince." What young Haitians who, like her own parents, found themselves living under the first Duvalier yearned for and seized when they could, Danticat goes on, was precisely "an art that could convince ... them that they would not die the same way that Numa and Drouin did ... that words could still be spoken, and that stories could still be told and passed on" (8).

As Danticat takes the occasion of the 1964 execution of Drouin and Numa as the touchstone for her elaborated reflections on what her 2010 essay subtitles "the Immigrant Artist at Work," the present essay takes Danticat's piece as its own corresponding touchstone in order to elaborate a theory of the literary act in contexts of interest and relevance to the field that currently calls itself US Latinx literary studies, and in ways that admittedly exceed any irreducibly specific, exclusive, defining or identifying relationship to that field. It matters here that, in choosing to open with a discussion of Danticat's work, the present essay insists already (as noted briefly above) on a historical, strategic and performative construction of "US Latinx," one that includes US-based immigrant communities from a "Latin" America that exceeds the Spanish-speaking regions originally colonized by Spain, and in addition that it will emphasize, without categorically insisting on, a construction of US Latinx literature as in large part though certainly not exclusively an "immigrant" literature, but where the "immigrant" status of the writer, and the potential spatial and temporal itinerancy of the text, rather than any depiction of immigrant "experience" in the work, will qualify actors and actions for inclusion in the field.[2] Danticat's account of the immigrant artist-writer in particular emphasizes both the existential stakes of any writing that imagines a world beyond what prevailing structures of power dictate to be possible, and proper, and in addition, how that writing bears witness to conditions of risk, and threat, and precarity, and contingency, specific to the writer who knows herself to be a newly landed, a perhaps even accidental, perhaps unauthorized, arrival to the linguistic, discursive, cultural and political realms where she might finally find a voice, a home and some effective cultural, social and political franchise.

Building on her observations about Haiti's Club de Bonne Humeur and their work with Camus, Danticat goes on:

> There were many recurrences of this story throughout the country, book and theatre clubs secretly cherishing some potentially subversive piece of literature, families burying if not burning entire libraries, books that might seem innocent but could easily betray them. Novels with the wrong titles. Treatises with the right titles and intentions. Strings of words that uttered, written or read, could cause a person's death. (9)

This quite historically specific scene of the production, performance, and circulation of discursive acts and imaginative, expressive material quickly broadens in Danticat's terms to a more general, even conceptual, construction of the scene of writing that matters to her:

> Create dangerously, for people who read dangerously. This is what I've always thought it meant to be a writer. Writing, knowing in part that no matter how trivial your words may seem, someday, somewhere, someone may risk his or her life to read them. Coming from where I come from, with the history that I have, ... this is what I've always seen as the unifying principle among all writers. (10)

Danticat's argument here, compellingly and fascinatingly, both rehearses *and* upends the by now 50-year-old French post-structural, postmodern deconstruction of the canonical author function, a critical genealogy that famously runs from Barthes' "Death of the Author" (1967) to Foucault's "What Is an Author?" (1969), and along the way also collects corollary contributions from thinkers as formidable and influential as Derrida ("Signature, Event, Context," 1972) and Lyotard (*The Postmodern Condition*, 1979). Against the traditional combined Enlightenment/Romantic construction of the literary genius-artist-author as present embodiment of the absolutely, fully realized subject of liberal Western modernity (both rational and creative, analytical and passionate, and fully, intentionally in control of and responsible for his [*sic*] creative activity and its creative productions), which this critical genealogy also opposes, Danticat proposes instead a construction of the *writer* in much more generally possible contexts, those that emphasize conditions of precarity, and of an existential, historical immanence so new and so potentially fleeting as to feel more like an evanescence, but where the creative will nevertheless assert itself enough to risk both the very event of that assertive utterance, and also the mortal consequence(s) that might, and in too many cases will almost certainly, follow. These contexts do not necessarily have to be explicitly political, let alone explicitly within contexts of totalitarian violence and censorship; they might, in fact, obtain wherever access to expression, and the sanction to express, remain unevenly, unjustly and interestedly distributed, and wherever whatever power prevails holds simultaneous and inter-implicated sway over who may write (let alone *speak*), and who may act (let alone *live*).[3]

Of all her French philosophical forebears whose work echoes in and through Danticat's, the one whose decades-old dismantling of everything that traditionally conceptually enabled the effects of writing and reading most directly bears on the work of the present essay is Jacques Derrida's in "Signature, Event, Context" (1972).[4] If in Danticat's terms writing and reading constitutively occur under conditions of both existential and political risk or threat, those conditions only intensify as they more specifically contextualize that fatal play of absence and presence that, according to Derrida, generally underwrites all acts of utterance, written or spoken. Like Danticat, who begins her reflections following the anecdote of the 1964 execution with the subversive work of Haiti's reading and drama groups, Derrida opens his analysis of existential precarity in the scene of writing with the reader:

> Could we maintain that, following the death of the receiver, or even of both partners, the mark left by one is still writing? Yes, to the extent that, organized by a code, even an unknown and non-linguistic one, it is constituted in its identity as mark by its iterability, in the absence of such and such a person, hence ultimately of every empirically determined "subject."
> ... To be what it is, all writing must, therefore, be capable of functioning in the radical absence of every empirically determined receiver in general. And this absence is not a continuous modification of presence, it is a rupture in presence, the "death" or the possibility of the "death" of the receiver inscribed in the structure of the mark. (7–8)

The logical jump is a short one from Derrida's general conceptual insistence on the existential precarity of any reader to Danticat's more historicized insistence on the very likely precarity (both political and existential) of any likely reader in whatever future a writer imagines any situated reception for her work. "Create dangerously," she commands, "for people who read dangerously"; again, like Derrida, Danticat insists here that an equivalent and corresponding condition of precarious risk befalls the writer. In Derrida's terms:

> What holds for the receiver holds also, for the same reasons, for the sender or producer. For a writing to be a writing it must continue to "act" and to be readable even when what is called the author of the writing no longer answers for what he has written, for what he seems to have signed, be it because of a temporary absence, because he is dead, or more generally,

> because he has not employed his absolutely actual and present intention
> or attention, the plenitude of his desire to say what he means, in order to
> sustain what seems to be written "in his name." (7–8)

In 2018, more than a decade since Jacques Derrida's actual death, these
lines necessarily resonate more emotionally than their decidedly rational,
analytical modality may have wanted in their own moment of articulation
to allow, but it is difficult not to hear in some of Derrida's own locu-
tions here (from the writer's guarded indifference to any given reader
as "such and such a person," but whose quite necessary indifference
ushers in the ontological crisis, the very "rupture in presence" itself that
Derrida's essay wants so clinically to explain, to the almost elegiac reference to what we lose with the equally dead author, that is, "the plenitude
of his desire to say what he means, ... to sustain what seems to be written 'in his name'") an aesthetic appreciation on his part of the dramatic
and affective force of his work here, and perhaps with some relation (we
dare to suggest) to his own biography. "Coming from where I come
from, with the history that I have," Danticat qualifies her assertions in
her own work, but only in order to return to a general ambition of assertion she shares with her fellow "immigrant" writer (Derrida) from the
larger space of a French colonial and imperial history that meaningfully
and violently implicates them both: "this is what I've always seen as the
unifying principle among all writers" (10).

As this section of the present essay concludes, a number of points can
emerge as relevant to the work that follows. First, to the extent that we
are participating in a larger conversation about a viable theory of the
ontology of the literary act, and of literary practice, the moments when
Derrida moves toward an articulation of writing's being matter here: we
will continue to bear in mind what, he argues, must obtain for "all writing" ... "[t]o be what it is"; how, in particular, "[f]or a writing to be a
writing, it must continue to 'act' ... " Second, we should not underes-
timate the importance of the "immigrant" itinerancy of the writing act
in the ways it makes sense to both Danticat and Derrida. For Danticat
certainly it is crucial that, as the life of the writer might always entail
an itinerancy that transports her from country to country, from home
to home, the afterlife of the text always entails an even more capacious
potential for circulation: "Somewhere," she muses, "if not now, then

maybe years in the future, we may also save someone's life, because they have given us a passport, making us honorary citizens of their culture … Even without globalization," she concludes, "the writer bound to the reader, under diabolic, or even joyful, circumstances inevitably becomes a loyal citizen of the country of his readers" (10, 15). For Derrida, that itinerancy takes on a more structural conceptualization, but (as the following passage shows) not without strategic figurations (the "drift" from responsible authorial consciousness that "orphans" writing from its "parent" intentional meaning) that anchor us in a decidedly personal, and not un-historical, drama: "This essential drift, bearing on writing as iterative structure, cut off from all absolute responsibility, from *conscious-ness* as the ultimate authority, orphaned and separated at birth from its father, is precisely what Plato condemns in the *Phaedrus*. If Plato's gesture," Derrida concludes, "is, as I believe, the philosophical gesture par excellence, one can measure what is at stake here" (8).[5] If Derrida's own move here is the deconstructive, anti-philosophical, anti-ontological gesture "par excellence," the one that finally puts the pale to any authority we might want to stake in the present being of any given writer, or reader, or whatever (metaphysical) truth or (transcendent) meaning either ever hoped to touch or to know so directly as to ignore the writing, the text, that actually makes all such promises and guarantees their necessary openness to failure, he does, in fact leave us with something, with what Danticat calls in her essay the "work." As later sections of the present essay will suggest, what might be occurring in 2018, more than a half-century since the murders of Drouin and Numa, and since the emergence in the United States and other parts of the world of the political, social, cultural, and intellectual conditions that brought both US Latinx literature, and US Latinx literary studies, to full and robust life, may appear to be a return to both philosophy and ontology (and in turn through them to an alternatively material history) that would seem either to disprove or at least reject the whole genealogy of post-structural, de-ontological deconstruction that Derrida inaugurates in work like "Signature, Event, Context," it may also be the case that Derrida among others, was not unknowingly setting the ground for a new analysis of the interaction of world and mind, and one that knows to put productive attention not on objects, or ends, or what passes for truth, but on process, and practice, and work.

NOTES

1. A very early draft of this section was written on October 4, 2014, the day that the world learned of the death of "Baby Doc" Jean-Claude Duvalier.

2. My assertions about a signature immigrant, itinerant cast to US Latinx literary practice should by no means suggest to the reader that I'm either ignoring, dismissing or downgrading work from or about historic, settled Latinx communities whose locations in US territory well-predate the moment when the US southern and western border(s) literally "*crossed them.*" The mobility, migrancy and itinerancy of texts, as well as of their writers and their readers, can take many forms in claiming their eligibility for, and legibility within, the "logic" of Latinx literary practice that I trace here. Indeed I hope this discussion can be read as welcoming an active conversation with such important historicist projects in the field, many extending their scope back before even the nineteenth century, and that include: Kirsten Silva Gruesz, *Ambassadors of Culture: The Transamerican Origins of Latino Writing* (Princeton UP, 2001); Rodrigo Lazo, *Writing to Cuba: Filibustering and Cuban Exiles in the United States* (University of North Carolina Press, 2005); Nicole M. Guidotti-Hernández, *Unspeakable Violence: Remapping U.S. and Mexican National Imaginaries* (Duke UP, 2011); Raúl Coronado, *A World Not to Come: A History of Latino Writing and Print Culture* (Harvard UP, 2013); Paula Moya, *The Social Imperative: Race, Close Reading, and Contemporary Literary Criticism* (Stanford UP, 2015); Rogrigo Lazo and Jesse Alemán, Eds., *The Latino Nineteenth Century* (New York UP, 2016); Jennifer Harford Vargas, *Forms of Dictatorship: Power, Narrative, and Authoritarianism in the Latina/o Novel* (Oxford UP, 2018); Ralph E. Rodriguez, *Latinx Literature Unbound: Undoing Ethnic Expectation* (Fordham UP, 2018); and Dixa Ramírez, *Colonial Phantoms: Belonging and Refusal in the Dominican Americas, from the 19th Century to the Present* (New York UP, 2018) (all Print).

3. This mostly conceptual comment on Danticat's general theory of the writer as a corrective of traditional theories of the author or artist can stand as stated here for the purposes of the discussion in this section, but readers interested in a more fully developed elaboration on Danticat's part of the mortal stakes of the forms of literacy and writing that emerge under conditions informed by accident, precarity, risk, and threat should consult the passages in her 2007 memoir *Brother, I'm Dying* where she narrates her own coming to literacy first in Haiti, then in the United States, in scenes where she depicts, for example, her serving while still a child in Haiti as the public interpreter of her father's handwritten letters in French to the family after his departure to the United States (21–24), and later, her receiving

the gift of a typewriter, from her father once she had settled into her new life and her new education in English in the United States (118–119).

4. Readers familiar with Derrida's essay will notice that my discussion devotes the bulk of its attention to only one of about four major critical movements in it, the one involving the dialectic of absence/presence of the writer and reader constitutive of the work of the graphematic mark (that is, of writing), and that it does so to emphasize some striking parallels to Danticat's characterization of the fatally dangerous work of writing, both in production and reception, in her essay. Those readers will also observe that the other movement in Derrida's essay of direct relevance to our work here has to do with his definitive critical deconstruction of J. L. Austin's claims regarding the perhaps ontologically performative force of certain kinds of utterance in *How to Do Things with Words*. In that passage Derrida argues the following, providing another important theoretical articulation of the event that guides much of our work here: "We should first be clear on what constitutes the status of 'occurrence' or the eventhood of the event that entails in its allegedly present and singular emergence the intervention of an utterance that in itself can be only repetitive or citational in its structure, or rather, since those two words may lead to confusion: iterable" (17–18). It will have to suffice here merely to suggest additional directions for reflection about the ways that one future thread of US Latinx literary studies might want to claim its own Derridean, deconstructive and post-structural influences, especially with respect to whatever additional claims it in turn wants to make about the *evental* or *eventive* ontological status of any literary act as utterance, as well as the status of a quality of ethnicity that might ground in some putative condition of object-hood claims to ethnic identity categories, like *latinidad*, on the part of any given individual subject or collective population.

5. Derrida's text in the original French bears reading here: "La situation du scripteur et du souscripteur est, quant à l'écrit, foncièrement la même que celle du lecteur. Cette dérive essentielle tenant à l'écriture comme structure iterative, coupée de toute responsabilité absolue, de la conscience comme autorité de dernière instance, orpheline et séparée dès sa naissance de l'assistance de son père, c'est bien ce que Platon condamnait dans le *Phèdre*. Si le geste de Platon est, comme je le crois, le movement philosophique par excellence, on mesure ici l'enjeu qui nous occupe." Derrida, *Marges de la Philosophie* (Paris: Éditions Minuit, 1975): 376.

CHAPTER 3

Archive and Diaspora:
Julia Alvarez as Poet, Novelist,
and Historian

Abstract "Archive and Diaspora" turns to work in the philosophy of history by Hayden White to underwrite a reading of the novelist, poet, and essayist Julia Alvarez that argues for her literary work's positive contributions to an unfolding readerly sense of Dominican, Caribbean, and Latinx-diasporic history. The section devotes serious attention to two of Alvarez's major works of historical fiction, the novels *In the Time of the Butterflies* and *In the Name of Salomé*, focusing on each text's distinct approach to deploying the resources of literature to do the work of history.

Keywords Feminism · History · Fiction · Archive · Diaspora · Genre · Event

In the concluding paragraph of "The Value of Narrativity in the Representation of Reality," the first chapter of his 1987 book *The Content of the Form*, Hayden White takes his fellow historians (whom he terms "the modern historiographical community") to task; he chides them for what he suggests was their willful blindness to the paradox at the heart of what passed then (as now?) for official, and legitimate, historiographical discourse. Especially in its embrace of a structuring, and definitive, narrativity, that discourse had, in spite of itself, indulged (White argues) in the kind of "moralizing judgment" that could bear no close scrutiny in the context of modern historiography's equally defining claims to have

© The Author(s) 2019
R. L. Ortiz, *Latinx Literature Now*, Literatures of the Americas,
https://doi.org/10.1007/978-3-030-04708-5_3

achieved the status of "a fully 'objective' discipline—a science of a special sort but a science nonetheless" (24). According to White, the historio-graphical establishment of his time had, in fact, absorbed into itself the capacity of assigning to the pseudo-scientific structuration of narrative per se an authoritative force more appropriate to its own institutional will-to-knowledge as opposed to, say, a more philosophical, or even literary, will-to-truth, or wisdom. Indeed, White goes on to say, this putatively sci-entific "value attached to narrativity in the representation of real events ar[ose] out of a desire to have real events display the coherence, integrity, fullness, and closure of an image of life that is and can only be imagi-nary." The notion, he concludes, "that sequences of real events possess the formal attributes of the stories we tell about imaginary events could only have its origin in wishes, daydreams, and reveries," the last of which are the only possible source of any expectation, individual or collective, of a historiographical (let alone *historical*) "coherence that permits us to see 'the end' in every beginning" (24).[1]

White mostly succeeds in this discussion at keeping at bay a certain, otherwise irresistible, comparison to the genre of literary fiction, which even despite his best efforts necessarily haunts the terminology of his pointed critique of modern historiography. This is understandable, to the extent that, arguably, the question of literary fiction certainly could remain only tangentially, or contingently, relevant to the conversation White proposes (practically, strategically) having exclusively with his fel-low historians. The closest that he comes to such an explicit invocation of that counter discourse to his own comes in his invocation of that "fic-tion of a world" which historiography mistakenly posits as "capable of speaking for itself and of displaying itself in the form of a story" in its efforts to produce the effect of a "realism in representation" that in turn authorizes it to speak as knowledge (25). And yet, the question of the literary does clearly haunt this conversation, and fuels in part the larger anxieties evident, on the one hand, in White's impatience with his his-torian colleagues, and, on the other, his grudging acknowledgment that certain emerging theoretical movements with deep roots in literary, linguistic, and philosophical criticism have necessarily come to bear on his own chosen discipline and its defining discursive practices. In some ways, White's 1987 invocation of "the imaginary" as a necessary criti-cal conceptualization of the narrative operations of modern historio-graphical discourse represents a pivotal moment in a larger genealogical elaboration, certainly very much alive in that period, bridging Lacanian,

Barthean, and Foucauldian post-structural theory with other similar work, such as Benedict Anderson's in *Imagined Communities* of the same decade, and Homi Bhabha's *Nation and Narration* of the decade after that, work which has in part addressed some of White's disciplinary anxieties by exploring the ways in which some discursive modes manage at once to be imaginary, historical, and capable of variously legitimate, and productive, claims to knowledge, andeven to truth.

The present discussion proposes tracing at least one such discursive genealogical node, that connecting the Dominican-American novelist and poet Julia Alvarez to SaloméUreña de Henríquez and Camila Henríquez Ureña, the chosen historical subjects of her 2000 historical novel, *In the Name of Salomé*, less to examine how the novel adequately (or not) represents any historical "reality" that it may claim to describe, and more to explore the ways that Alvarez's literary solicitation of those subjects constitutes an historical act, comprises an historical performative that necessarily (and knowingly) *makes* as much "history" as it purports to tell. By the time Alvarez publishes *Salomé* in 2000, she had already distinguished herself as a prolific literary writer, as both novelist and poet, and as a versatile practitioner of distinct narrative modes, having published three major novels, two that fictionalized her own immigrant family's experiences of cultural assimilation into and political negotiation with the dominant culture of their host country, and one that established her skill with historical fiction. That novel, 1994's *In the Time of the Butterflies*, told in fictional form the story of the Mirabal sisters, nicknamed *las mariposas* by the Dominican public who supported their efforts in the organized underground resistance against the dictator Trujillo in the course of the 1940s and 1950s; three of the *mariposas* were murdered by Trujillo's thugs in 1960, and by the 1990's they were official national heroines in the Dominican Republic, though not well known in the United States. In *Butterflies*, Alvarez does a number of things that help her reader not only situate her fiction in its informing historical context, but also mark her own active participation in the production of her immediate text, as well as in the generation of a further discursive network exceeding what she herself personally engenders.

For example, she inserts a version of herself into the novel's narration by inventing an interlocutor , significantly a *"gringa dominicana"* writer who comes to the DR in the 1990's to interview Bélgica (Dedé) Mirabal, the surviving *mariposa*, about her heroic martyr sisters (3). In addition, she includes at the end of her novel a "Postscript" that briefly

describes her methods of investigating the lives of the sisters and of trans-
lating the results of that research into the novel in her readers' hands.
While her account in the novel itself gives some indication of Alvarez's
interactions with both Dedé and Minou, the daughter of Minerva
Mirabal, the "Postscript" adds the necessary caveat to any reader of the
novel concerning its status as an act of invention; "as happens with any
story," Alvarez warns us, "the characters took over, beyond polemics and
beyond facts. They became real to my imagination. I began to invent
them" (323). The contrast here between Hayden White's profound anxiety concerning modern historiography's disqualifying debt to a narrative
impulse rooted in "wishes, daydreams and reveries" and Alvarez's com-
fort in what she claims to be fiction's alternative historiographical authority couldn't be more stark, or more telling. She admits, on the one hand,
that she resisted merely reviving "the sisters of legend, wrapped in super-
latives and ascended into myth" because "such deification was dangerous, the same god-making impulse that had created our dictator"; on the
other, she fully admits to taking "liberties" with historical fact, explaining
that she "wanted to immerse my readers in an epoch in the life of the
Dominican Republic that I believe can only finally be redeemed by the
imagination. A novel is not," she concludes, "a historical document, but
a way to travel through the human heart" (324).

One can certainly hear in such a reference to that "heart" some echo
of the kind of mystifying, interiorizing psychologism or moralism that
White so acutely and critically resists in *The Content of the Form*, but
Alvarez's repudiation of any claims to anything like historical authority
(let alone veracity) for her novel should not for this reason be taken as
either disturbingly naïve or annoyingly disingenuous. In both her narrative insertion of the *gringa dominicana* interlocutor and in other statements that she makes in both the "Postscript" and an essay she published
later entitled "Chasing the Butterflies," Alvarez clearly demonstrates an
understanding, as critical and knowing as White's, about the kinds of
claims, to knowledge and to truth, that her own historical project can
safely, and plausibly, make. On the one hand, she acknowledges that
what information about the Mirabal sisters she can expect her readers to
glean from her representation of them in the novel does not necessarily
have to lead to some greater *knowledge* about the sisters so much as to
further political action that uses some additional "acquaintance of these
famous sisters" as a strategic "model," especially for "women fighting
against injustices of all kinds" (324). On the other, Alvarez concludes

her "Postscript" by addressing "Dominicans separated by language from the world I have created" (324), meaning (presumably) Dominicans who cannot read English because they remained on the island, although perhaps she might extend this to all Dominicans who continue to suffer from illiteracy; either way, what Alvarez also acknowledges in such statements is the extent of a growing and increasingly complex Dominican diaspora, one in which she and her family participated when they fled Trujillo's terror in 1960, and one to which she has contributed so productively, discursively in the acts of fiction writing which make up the matter of the presentdiscussion.

In the "Chasing the Butterflies" essay, Alvarez develops further, and in deceptively informal terms, her understanding of the complex historical and discursive dynamics informing her retelling of the Mirabal sisters' stories. First, she acknowledges her own family's indirect personal connection to the women through her father's own participation in the same resistance movement against Trujillo, then her family's situation in the North American Dominican diaspora as a result of her father's decision to flee the DR just months before the *mariposas* were murdered (197). The sisters therefore come to haunt Alvarez personally because, as she tells it, they "stood in stark contrast to the self-saving actions of my own family and of other Dominican exiles" (198). Alvarez's opportunity to address this haunting shame came decades later when, in 1986, she was commissioned by what she calls "a women's press" to contribute to a postcard series about Latina women "a paragraph about a Dominican heroine of my choice"; to her dismay, the only book she could find dedicated to the sisters' story was "a historical 'comic book,'" featuring the "heroines with balloons coming out of their mouths" (199). In her attempts to uncover what she calls more "formal information" about the *mariposas*, Alvarez narrates the process that turned eventually into her near-decade of research into their lives and the history of their nation, research that led her not only to such first-hand sources as Dedé and her niece Minou (daughter of Minerva Mirabal and her husband Manolo Tavárez), but also to other variously "archival" resources as the museum built in the sisters' honor at the site of the family home in Salcedo, the yellowing copies of the newspaper *El Caribe* dating back to the week of the murders and held at the Dominican National Archives, and finally documents as personal as Minerva and Manolo Tavárez's love letters to one another "written [Alvarez tells us] during their many separations, [a] mong them, letters they had smuggled back and forth in prison" (201).

All of this intensely intimate research across all spheres of a family's and a nation's historical life prompts Alvarez's decision, finally, to opt for fiction over history or biography as the most appropriate mode for going on with her work. Her explanation for this decision varies, however, from the one she offers in her "Postscript" to the novel concerning her desire to guide her readers on a journey "through the human heart." The essay's explanation indulges perhaps an alternative sentimentality to that informing the "Postscript," but in other ways it addresses more directly and in more sober and critical form some of the issues that worried White about representation and the historical as defining problems for historians. "[A]fter I wrote my Latina postcard paragraph," Alvarez confesses, "I put the project away. The story seemed to me too impossible to write. It was too perfect, too tragic, too awful. The girls' story didn't need a story. And besides, I couldn't yet imagine how one tells a story like this. *Once upon a holocaust, there were three butterflies.* A paragraph of this stuff was quite enough" (202). Alvarez here shrewdly and rather audaciously takes on the whole project of historical representation in ways that Hayden White was perhaps too modest, if not too timid, to attempt, but in ways that mainly underscore rather than undermine his critique. First, she acknowledges that even in the most informally archivized form, the materials she consulted always already availed themselves, whether directly or indirectly, of some quality of narrativity; whether she focuses on the braid of María Teresa's haircut from her corpse and displayed under glass at the museum (200), or on the ruins of Patria Mercedes and Pedrito Gonzáles' farmhouse near Salcedo (206), or on the possible visual representation of the ambush on the mountain road that locals near that site imagine in some future film version (209), Alvarez at every step in her research finds herself "touch[ing] history" (207) in a manner that insists on, even as it capitulates to, a narrativity always already imbedded in what she calls in the passage just quoted "this stuff." And second, that structural inevitability is exactly what challenges her to negotiate with, rather than to decry, the fictionalizing tendency of all narrative, even if it means (in two of the more extreme—to her—manifestations she invokes in the essay) imagining the Mirabal matter narrated either as a comic book or (a rather perverse) fairytale (i.e., "*Once upon a holocaust ...* ").

At this point the present discussion will turn from *In the Time of the Butterflies* to Alvarez's second and in some ways more ambitious attempt to excavate Dominican national and cultural history with the help of a decidedly fictionalizing discursive apparatus, this time in her 2000 novel *In the Name of Salomé*. If already in *Butterflies* Alvarez's work could be described as not merely "representing" history via a second-order, recomposed and passively verbal account of a sequence or confluence of historical events (however creatively or imaginatively) culled from a variety of "primary" or more conventionally "archival" sources, but in fact as participating actively and critically in an ongoing discursive operation devoted to a more fully and heterogeneously elaborated historical archivization of the Mirabal (and hence Dominican) matter, then in the later novel the attribution of such a historical force to the writer's work can only be said to be deepened and further complicated. On the one hand, while in *Butterflies* the connection between Alvarez and her subjects remained (however powerful) logically contingent, and metonymic, to the extent that they each found themselves implicated in an unfolding Dominican and Dominican-diasporic national narrative organized around the Trujillo dictatorship, in *Salomé* Alvarez encounters subjects with whom she enjoys differently powerful, because conceptual and metaphoric, relations. Like Salomé Ureña, the iconic national poet of the DR in its late nineteenth century period of nascent and troubled sovereignty, Alvarez is herself a poet as well, and is therefore situated not only in a common historical context, but in a more specific, and evocative, cultural and literary genealogy with her subject. Alvarez recalls that while her own initiation into the writing life had "begun in poetry," what she learned while "growing up and going to college and reading the canon" did not include texts by nonwhite, nonAnglo writers; "these stories," she recounts in an interview published with the paperback edition of *Salomé*, "were–if present at all—considered 'sociology,' not literature, never fully credentialed."[2]

Her research into the life and work of Salomé Ureña therefore implicates Alvarez and her own work quite differently than her research into the Mirabal matter could have. "I have to smile when I think," Alvarez goes on in the same interview, "that one hundred years after her death in 1897, Salomé Ureña, the great educator of Dominican women, was teaching me my history and native language through her poems and letters." And beyond this question of Alvarez's inheritance of a literary patrimony from her subject, of course, lies the related question of her eligibility to transport Salomé's work more fully into the diasporic, transnational space(s) in which Alvarez and her work find themselves more authentically if not comfortably at home. But as Alvarez herself is quick to point out, however, Salomé's early domestic reputation was based on "a few of her patriotic poems," which, because "they were considered '*varonil*,' i.e., masculine and weighty, were the ones that were celebrated" by her contemporaries; these poems are not, Alvarez goes on, "her best in my opinion," and it was only with the publication in 1996 of an *Epistolario* containing letters from the entire Henríquez Ureña clan that a Dominican reading audience could finally appreciate the "living, suffering woman" behind the less canonical "poems about her family, her feelings for [her husband] Pancho" favored by Alvarez. In either case, Ureña's body of work offers Alvarez little in the way of formal models or convivial themes, and it also offers little for a poet with her skill set in the way of possible sources for exercises in translation.

What Ureña does offer Alvarez, of course, is the opportunity to explore in a decidedly different historical and cultural context what can remain in the most recently passing *fin-de-siècle* period of the figure of the literary writer as national mouthpiece, a figure still so prevalent and influential in the immediately preceding centennial turn. As Alvarez herself has observed, "[b]y the time she was seventeen, Salomé had become the republic's national icon on the strength of her fiercely patriotic poems for 'la patria,' or the homeland. Her words sparked unprecedented passion, gave voice to countless disenfranchised countrymen, and assumed a central role in motivating the fight for independence, whether from Spain or Haiti." WhileUreña never physically left the Dominican Republic, her career as represented by Alvarez in her novel nevertheless opens her up to a more contemporary transnational analysis that can draw from scholarly and theoretical work like Kirsten Silva Gruesz's in her 2002 book *The Ambassadors of Culture*, on what Gruesz calls the "*Transamerican Origins of Latino Writing*". Indeed, much can be made beyond the space of the present discussion regarding the felicitous appearance of Gruesz's foundational work two years after Alvarez's novel. Certainly it makes sense that, given Gruesz's focus on US Latinx writing in the nineteenth century, she would never have occasion to mention such an island-bound figure as Salomé Ureña, but Alvarez's novel beautifully anticipates and complements Gruesz's scholarship by introducing into its narrative world such transnationalized figures as Eugenio María de Hostos, who spent considerable time in Salomé's Santo Domingo cultural and political circles, and José Martí, who makes a brief appearance in the novel, but whose work is as profoundly influential to its characters' thinking as it is central to the argument of Gruesz's book.

One could, for example, hear in Gruesz's account of what she calls the "Romantic-era search for the national author whose writing would best represent 'our' essential values and character ... [as it] sought to compress a complex web of meanings into a single icon of cultural mastery" almost an ideal coda for the narrative of Salomé's life as told by Alvarez (15); how much more perfect, then, that in a parenthetical aside in that very sentence Gruesz observes that "this is a process one also sees at work in the contemporary context of ethnic writers" (15). And, in fact, one need not leap too far from Alvarez's observation in the interview quoted earlier that "Salomé was one of the most revered poets of the Dominican Republic, 'la musa de la patria,'" to her interviewer's corresponding observation that no "other author writing in English" had done more than Julia Alvarez "to raise the consciousness of United States readers about the rich culture of the Dominican Republic and to document the country's tragic, exceptionally volatile history across the last two centuries." One certainly should pause here to hear the strong echo of "musa de la patria" in what was just articulated regarding a "musa de la diáspora" whose difference from the former might be more a question of context than inherence.

What remains of the present discussion will briefly take up one particularly evocative episode in *Salomé* which confirms Alvarez's clear sense of her own participation in a historical genealogical elaboration, no less material for being discursive, at least as old as the nineteenth century, and as recently revisited and reconfigured as the turn into a twenty first century that has seen the near-simultaneous publication of her novel and Gruesz's study. The episode takes place in 1892, late in the novel, and late in Salomé's life, but at a pivotal moment in a longer transamerican history in which the novel strategically situates itself. That year Salomé finds herself in retreat to improve her health in the northern coastal town of Puerto Plata; because she's not in Santo Domingo, she can only hear "rumors of the preparations going on in the capital for the Columbus celebrations" (268). 1892, marking the 400-year anniversary of the inauguration of New World history, is especially significant to Dominican national culture, which identifies itself perhaps more intimately with the whole complex Columbian legacy than any other Caribbean nation does. Alvarez of course has Salomé observe that, at least in the immediate Dominican context, the anniversary celebrations suffer from their significant juxtaposition with the atrocities committed in the same weeks and months by Ulisis (Lilís) Hereaux, the Dominican dictator *du jour*. Rumor, Salomé recounts, tells her that "as the Niña, Pinta and Santa María replicas sent by Spain entered our harbor, they floated on the sea along with the bodiesof Lilís' enemies" (268).

The retreat both manages to restore Salomé's health, and to revive her creative drive after a long hiatus, and she reports writing two poems ("¡Tierra!" and "Fe") for the occasion of the Columbian celebration, and whose early careers as public texts are narrated in the following passage:

> I sent both poems to Pancho, and of course he chose "¡Tierra!" to read at the concluding celebration. If I am to believe Pancho's account of the evening, my poem was well received. At the end of the ceremonies at the Teatro Republicano, Pancho stood and recited it, hand tucked in his frock coat, no doubt, and using that slight French accent he refused to lose. The great apostle Martí, the great general Máximo Gómez, and the incomparable Meriño, and the next president Marchena (Pancho's superlatives!) had all been visibly moved. Even Martí took out his handkerchief. Pancho swore it was the power of my poetry, but I imagine that the apostle was thinking of his own dear Cuba from which he had been exiled for so many years.
>
> "¡Mi musa, mi esposa, mi amor, mi tierra!" Pancho closed. (269–270)

This remarkable passage requires much more explication than the present discussion can devote to it. Suffice it to say here that Alvarez, in situating her heroine as both present and absent in the scene of her poem's recital in the capital, understands clearly the historical stakes of participating in a fully politically committed act of literary expression, an act that simultaneously points toward and away from its chosen historical referents. Whatever one might want to say about the accuracy or veracity of the representation of this extraordinary gathering of historical figures in Santo Domingo's Teatro Republicano in 1892, much can be said about (for example) the authenticity, and force, of Alvarez's observation, through Salomé, of the profound, albeit sentimental, nationalist ties binding her verses to what she imagines motivates Martí's tears.

A more extensive version of this discussion might have turned next to Alvarez's parallel narration of Salomé's daughter Camila's life story in the same novel; Camila, who both lives most of her life outside the DR, primarily in Cuba and the United States, and struggles in the course of that life with her lesbianism, also both realizes something of the (admittedly difficult) promise of the inter-American transnationalism already present in the scene just discussed, and embodies that realized promise in a way that posits her as something like a "queer mother" for an inter-American transnation always remaining to be imagined. Such extended work could also revisit the question of the archive, especially, as famously contraposed with a competing conceptualization of a performative repertoire by Diana Taylor, to worry the logical claims of such a contraposition. What, that discussion would have to ask, prevents the logical identification, and reactivation, of what is arguably "repertorial" in any archive, or archival in any repertoire? This last question, a version of which may also haunt similarly recent theoretical elaborations of the testimonial contraposed with literary modes of historical witnessing, will bring the present discussion back around to the linguistic, discursive, ontological, and epistemological themes raised by its initial invocation of Hayden White. The following section will instead take a different approach in reading how Camila matters to the questions posed here, allowing us to reintroduce John Beverley to the conversation, and to expand our engagement with historical philosophy by introducing work by Michel-Rolphe Trouillot's that both responds to and departs from Hayden White's.

Notes

1. According to Ilai Rowner, "If history could be called the art of the event's sense, then literature would be the artistic effort of the event's non-sense. If history demands what exactly has taken place in any given moment of the past, literary inquiry aspires for the non-place of the taking place: what is there in the event that does not reveal itself exactly in the happening." Such important recent work extends the thread of conceptual elaboration traced in the main essay through our readings of Derrida, White, Trouillot, and Eagleton. See Ilai Rowner, *The Event: Theory and Literature* (University of Nebraska Press, 2015): 12. Print.
2. See   http://us.penguingroup.com/static/rguides/us/name_of_salome. html. Website accessed 15 April 2007.

CHAPTER 4

Against *Against Literature*: Histories of Fiction, Fictions of History

Abstract This section combines several threads of discussion from previous sections, including bringing Alvarez more directly into conversation with Danticat, introducing work in the philosophy of history by Michel-Rolphe Touillot to deepen the earlier analysis of Hayden White, and returning to John Beverley's work on literature, testimonio, and cultural studies, to describe literature's, and literary studies', historical resilience in the face of especially Beverley's important critiques from the nineteen nineties. The section concludes by turning briefly to Alvarez's novel *Salomé* and Danticat's literary memoir *Brother, I'm Dying*, in order to describe how each text deploys literary resources to cut across and even to merge the mimetic registers of fiction and history.

Keywords Literary studies · Testimonio · Cultural studies · Historical fiction · Literary memoir · Blackness

As the preceding section briefly sketched, *In the Name of Salomé*, Julia Alvarez's ambitious historical novel published in 2000, traces the lives of Salomé Ureña de Henríquez, the national poet of the Dominican Republic in its early decades of shaky existence as a sovereign nation from the mid-nineteenth century on, and Camila Henríquez Ureña, Salomé's only daughter, who was just three years old when her mother died in 1897, and who lived most of her life in Cuba and in the United States until her death in 1973. *Brother, I'm Dying*, Edwidge Danticat's

© The Author(s) 2019
R. L. Ortiz, *Latinx Literature Now*, Literatures of the Americas,
https://doi.org/10.1007/978-3-030-04708-5_4

2007 literary memoir, is set primarily in the year 2004, which saw both the deaths of her father and her paternal uncle, the two men the writer credits with raising her, and the birth of her own first child. Father and uncle serve Danticat in her memoir much as mother and daughter serve Alvarez in her novel; each pair of characters provides each writer with a rich opportunity for engaging in complex, productive forms of narrative strategy, and narrative practice. The narrative structure organizing events in Alvarez's novel is the more straightforwardly schematic of the two; *Salomé* parallels chapters following the title character's experiences as a teenage girl in mid-nineteenth century Santo Domingo to her death from tuberculosis at century's end, with chapters tracing Camila's life roughly backward, from her retirement from a teaching position at Vassar in the early 1960s to her earliest experiences in the Dominican Republic during her ailing mother's last years of life. The overall narrative effect of reading *Salomé* through is one of symmetrical, reciprocal temporal and historical convergence, the narrative endpoint arriving as a historical midpoint, that moment in the late 1890s when mother and daughter share three brief years of a common existence. Danticat's memoir opens and closes in 2004, but in its intervening chapters it completes its larger narrative of familial, national and diasporic histories by reaching back as far as colonial Hispaniola, and devoting a great deal of attention to especially twentieth-century Haitian history; because Danticat's father Miracin left Haiti for diasporic life in the United States in the early 1970s, much of the narrative of island Haitian life in *Brother, I'm Dying* revolves around her uncle Joseph, both in the years he spent caring for Danticat and one of her brothers during their parents' absence, and in the years following Danticat's own departure to the Brooklyn, NY, which became her Haitian diasporic home in 1981.

I want to use this brief exposition of what I'll call the comparative energies driving the narrative dialectics of Alvarez's and Danticat's texts in order to ground in some perhaps more discrete, concrete form an analysis of some related sets of perhaps more thematic, symbolic, and discursive dialectical energies I see emanating from the complex textual structures I just described. I do not claim to privilege one set of tensions over any other, and their necessary, instrumental, categorical differentiation here should not at all suggest that I've concluded that they're therefore literally separable from one another on a practical level. Working as I do here with a piece of literary historical fiction whose central characters are all meant to refer in fairly direct ways to actually once-existing historical persons, and with a literary memoir that is as attentive to its own operations as discursive gesture and practice as it is to the more conventional task of narrating as factually as it can the lives of its own actually historically existing characters, I am interested in exploring here to the extent possible the larger discursive tensions imbedded in either text in any case, but arguably intensified by the two texts' direct juxtaposition: the dialectics I have in mind here are those we might locate between the still-arguably archival practices of writing literary fiction and writing literary memoir on the one hand, and between the kinds of discursive, and archival, claims that might viably emanate from the work of literature, and the work of history, on the other.

Clearly, however, the dialectical tensions do not end at the level of discourse and knowledge as I so far construe it here. *In the Name of Salomé* and *Brother, I'm Dying* comprise a much more complex, robust object of analysis than that: as parallel attempts to retrieve and recount in literary form significant periods in the histories of the Dominican Republic and Haiti, they arguably participate in the tense binational dialectic that continues to inform political and cultural life on the island of Hispaniola; as narratives written from distinct diasporic locations on the US mainland, they in turn problematize whatever conventions of national historical narration they might invoke or even deploy by always framing those conventions within the larger, more complex transnational contexts shaped by the demands of the global imperial projects in play across the last two centuries, as well as the various aftermaths of displacement and dislocation those projects compel; given that the novel takes on the task of reimagining in order to re-narrate the experiences of two mixed race women who led quite public lives already available in and to the historical record, and given that the memoir brings the lives of two comparably private black men into a more public record thanks in part to the eventual notoriety of the young woman writer they raised and her decision to tell their story, these texts also pose quite powerfully a set of questions about genre, gender, class, and race which this essay will not have the time to address. But I do want to insist here on the work that these many nonconcentric circles of strategic acts of dialectical pairing do to mark the complex object of analysis before us as decidedly Hispaniolan-diasporic in a way that allows for a coding of "Hispaniolan-diasporic" that means a process of productive, and decidedly literary, deconstruction of any prevailing logics of (for starters) nation, and state, and empire.

I want to pause here first to insist on what I see as the significantly *literary* ground for the work that Alvarez and Danticat do together. As far back now as 1993, John Beverley could publish a book with a title as polemical as *Against Literature*, and there still invoke a notion of literature's "privilege[d]" status as what he calls a "signifier of the desire for a more egalitarian, democratic and economic social order" (xiv); "my intention," Beverley goes on to declare about his book, is "to produce a negation of the literary that would allow non-literary forms of cultural practice to displace its hegemony" (1).[1] The two "non-literary forms of cultural practice" that Beverley will propose and then champion as alternatives to literature are *testimonio* and cultural studies, and as readers familiar with either Beverley's scholarship or with developments in politically engaged humanities work over the past two decades will know, one of these has perhaps fared better than the other, but in any case, and certainly in the context of humanities-inflected American or Latinx Studies in its most recent iterations, no one currently should be too concerned with any looming hegemonic threat that literature or literary studies might pose, especially to interdisciplinary cultural studies. To his credit, Beverley takes a fairly even-handed approach in his polemic "against" literature; as early as the preface to the book we find him both asserting and moderating his central claim:

> In something that is so obviously connected via the education system to the state and to the formation of elites, there is always the danger that even the most iconoclastic and "progressive" literature is simply forging the new forms of hegemony. On the other hand, I do not think that there is some more privileged or effective space for the constitution of a politics of resistance or counter-hegemony than the education system itself, and it is difficult to imagine a human future in which variants of what we now know as literature will not play some role in the definition of new forms of human liberation and possibility. (xiv)[2]

Beverley's work can serve here as a useful measure of where culture and the scholarship of culture has come in the quarter century since it appeared; indeed, we can wonder if the "variants of what we now know as literature" might include, thanks in fact to work like Beverley's, all the modes of practice in, say, cinema, performance, and new media that cultural studies as a scholarly project has captured for critique and for knowledge in that time, although at the same time we might want to retain some space of viable operation for a practice that looks decidedly not like a "variant of what we now know as literature," but that pretty much still looks, and works, like, well, *literature*.

It is certainly no coincidence that Beverley turns to Pedro Henríquez Ureña himself, Salomé's son and Camila's brother, as the embodiment of what went wrong in literary studies, at least, but arguably not exclusively, in the Latin American studies context. Beverley calls Henríquez "the founder of modern Latin American literary criticism," and the authoritative purveyor of the argument that, since "the writing of the colonial and independence periods was a cultural practice that model[ed] the national, [this made] literature and literary values the key signifiers of regional identity for a national-bourgeois intelligentsia, [thus allowing those values to become] institutionalized as part of the ideology of the humanities in the Latin American university system" (3). We can at this point wonder first how best to accommodate the dynamic of relations informing literary study to the education system to the state in the Latin American contexts that matter here to Beverley and Henríquez to those prevailing across and even after the twentieth century in the United States, and wonder second if the experiences of populations migrating across national and regional spaces in the new world, and here embodied by Alvarez, Danticat, and the many historically based characters populating their narratives, have so altered and modified those relations now for so many decades that they render such conventional distinctions across nations and regions in our own day rather moot. But Beverley's invocation of Henríquez is interesting for other reasons in the context of the present discussion; Beverley maintains an admirably strict distinction between literature and literary studies as historical processes from literature's expressive content. He is, we might say, more interested (at least in these passages from his book) in literature in its institutional, or performative, rather than its expressive, or constative, mode(s). His interests lie more with literature's work rather than with its claims, although later in his opening chapter he will also complicate his primary argument by confessing that, rather than calling for a "supplantation" of literature in favor of *testimonio* and cultural studies, he will settle for "a more agnostic posture toward it, a way of problematizing it in the very act of teaching it in its disciplinary location" (21).

"Agnostic" might strike us as a pivotally, productively ambiguous term here. It allows for the simultaneous, skeptical resistance to perhaps the two ways one might be challenged to "believe" in literature; Beverley, we have already noted, primarily stays on the side of questioning adherence to what he sees as literature's instrumental (and more obviously historical) role in subtending larger, more practical forces of political, social, and cultural dominance, but we might then ask to what extent this agnosticism should also be directed toward the other claim that literature can make for a kind of practical credibility, not toward any claim of veracity for its obviously invented fictions, but perhaps a claim for a kind of serious, committed, critical regard for alternative kinds of (even historical, even epistemological) work that such fictiveness might nevertheless do? Two years after the appearance of *Against Literature*, the Haitian-American anthropologist Michel-Rolphe Trouillot published *Silencing the Past: Power and the Production of History* (1995), a collection of essays reflecting, in quite complementary ways to Beverley's on literature, on the complex work of historiography, and theories of historical knowledge in what we might call the post-Hayden White, post-Michel Foucault era. While no one would call Trouillot an "agnostic" about what he insists is always a "necessary" distinction between narratives that do the work of "history" from those that do the work of "fiction," his analysis of the process by which such distinctions come endlessly to be made and remade does provide us with language that complicates and expands further Beverley's more limited analysis of the kind of "historical" and "epistemological" work that literature might claim, work that we might want literature to do.

Like Beverley's, Trouillot's argument in "The Power in the Story," the opening chapter to *Silencing the Past*, both insists on the basic terms of its polemic, at the same time that it resists some of the polemic's potentially most uncompromising conclusions. "The need for a certain credibility," Trouillot argues, "sets the historical narrative apart from fiction. This need," he goes on, "is both contingent and necessary" (8). Trouillot's explanation of the relation of contingency to necessity deserves the following long quotation:

> It is contingent inasmuch as some narratives go back and forth over the line between fiction and history, while others occupy an undefined position that seems to deny the very existence of such a line. It is necessary inasmuch as, at some point, historically specific groups of humans must

decide if a particular narrative belongs to history or to fiction. In other words, the epistemological break between history and fiction is always expressed concretely through the historically situated evaluation of specific narratives. (8)

The logic driving Trouillot's main distinction here buckles fairly readily under the weight of its own self-deconstructing force. The contingency/ necessity dialectic quickly reveals itself as always already a double or a decoy for the fiction/history distinction it claims to want to adjudicate. One might ask, for example, why narratives that either, as Trouillot puts it, "go back and forth over the line between fiction and history" or indeed "deny the very existence of such a line" would ever, in that punctual moment of historical necessity when "historically specific groups of humans" face their necessary obligation to "decide if a particular narrative belongs to history or to fiction," do anything other than responsibly categorize such narratives of contingency as anything other than fiction? All the rest, at least as described here, in Trouillot's articulation of necessity is, we might say, *history*.

Trouillot's language describing the process of determining the historical credibility of some narratives over others is richly suggestive beyond the complex paradoxes of its core logic. His clearly intentionally vague characterization of "historically specific groups of humans" leaves open the question of the logic of the grouping itself; certainly from his own position in a Caribbean-, Hispaniolan-, Haitian diasporic-US, Trouillot may be exhibiting an understandable sensitivity to the responsibility that certain displaced "groupings" of "humans," those, say, without recourse to, but also therefore liberated from, the compelling demands of established national and even imperial, narratives, might take on in determining which narratives about themselves qualify as fiction, and which qualify as history. In addition, the move from the personified "groups of humans" exercising historical agency in one sentence to the characterization of a process of "historically situated evaluation" in the next also bears notice, if only because it opens a further space of distinction that will become relevant to some of the work that Trouillot goes on to do in the chapter in question. Finally, the locution Trouillot uses to describe the result of the process of discursive taxonomy opens an additional space of ambiguity thanks to the additional connotations we might ascribe to relations of "belonging." Certainly, no one doubts the logical, practical possibility that "historically specific groups of humans" do quite successfully, and quite responsibly, and quite often, "decide" which narratives about themselves "belong" to history, and which "belong" to fiction; but we also do not doubt that, in ways that we cannot ignore, fiction itself belongs decidedly to history, and history cannot ever fully claim that it has not at least in part belonged, and indeed to this day continues to belong, to fiction.

For those of us working in literary studies, projects like Trouillot's can invite further productive reflection on the promise that interdisciplinary scholarship still holds. If, as Trouillot suggests, "theories of history" suffer from their "rather limited view of the field of historical production, ... [its] size, ... [and] relevance, [and of] the complexity of the overlapping sites where history is produced, notably outside of academia" (19), literary scholarship might in some ways offer itself up as a resource in the mapping for knowledge of a "field of historical production" complex enough to include not only the kind of work of that journalists, documentarians and independent scholars might be doing "outside of academia," but also the contributions that writers of literary memoir, literary biography and historical fiction (among other relevant genres) might also make to the larger project at hand. Later in "The Power in the Story" Trouillot argues that "history reveals itself only through the production of specific narratives," and that "[w]hat matters most are the process and conditions of production of such narratives," and finally that "[o]nly through that overlap" between the material historical process itself, and the production of narratives about that process, "can we discover the differential exercise of power that makes some narratives possible and silences others" (25). Trouillot's recourse to an analysis of power as it drives the primarily material process of historical unfolding offers literary scholarship a larger, more open gesture of invitation to productively critical interdisciplinary work, if we attend strategically to his characterization of the simultaneous production of both articulated narrative and dis-articulated silence as the sibling offsprings of power's work in and on the world. "The production of traces," Trouillot reminds us, "is always also the production of silences ... What happened leaves traces, some of which are quite concrete—buildings, dead bodies, censuses, monuments, diaries, political boundaries—that limit the range and significance of any historical narrative. This is one of the many reasons," he concludes, "why not any fiction can pass for history" (29). Fair enough, but this should also not preclude the possibility that fiction in general, and perhaps literary practice more broadly construed, might nevertheless meaningfully and productively participate in the work of what Trouillot more expansively maps as the "field of historical production."[3]

One possible site of intervention for literary contributions to the work of responsible historical production lies, I want to argue here, precisely in that space of silence that Trouillot names for us: not silence as a pure space of failure or absence or lack, but silence as a potent, urgent space for future articulation, a space vital and alive as expectant possibility and potentiality. This, then, is where our pair of literary texts might briefly re-enter the conversation. Early in the narrative of *In the Name of Salomé*, Alvarez imagines the elderly Camila Henríquez's last days teaching Spanish language and literature at Vassar; in a sentimental mood thanks to her impending retirement, Camila decides to do something she's resisted doing over the years, sharing some of her mother Salomé's poems with her students. The pedagogical experiment fails; as one student observes, "They're too bewailing, o woe is me and my poor suffering country. 'And martyrdom beneath the fecund palms'! Is this poet supposed to be any good? I never heard of her," to which Camila snaps angrily, "As good as your Emily Dickinson, as good as your Walt Whitman" (39). Later that day, her rage having subsided, Camila has a moment to reflect about the tense scene of instruction. Alvarez writes: "Still, as she walks home, she cannot forget the indifference in their voices, the casualness of their dismissal. Everything of ours—from lives to literature—has always been so disposable, she thinks ... She smells her anger—it has a metallic smell mixed with earth, a rusting plow driven into the ground" (39). Something of Alvarez's larger expressive and critical project as a writer finds itself distilled in a passage like this, and in ways that Trouillot's analysis of the larger historical dialectic of traces and silences helps us to describe. Alvarez's turn to the language of disposability, of indifference and dismissal, to describe here the larger imperial attitude toward that "everything of ours—from lives to literature," that suffers historical silencing in both imperial and non-imperial spaces, turns as well toward what the rest of her novel offers as its own decidedly fictive but for that reason no less historical intervention into and against those processes of silencing. We see this as early as the decidedly literary turn toward figuration in the writer's imagistic, poetic description of Camila's anger: its "metallic smell mixed with earth, a rusting plow driven into the ground."[4]

Edwidge Danticat, roughly a generation younger than Alvarez though by 2007 that saw the appearance of *Brother, I'm Dying* finding herself in the middle of an extraordinary literary and public career, approaches Trouillot's dialectic of traces and silences in a manner that complements Alvarez's. In the "Create Dangerously" essay, first discussed two sections above, Danticat has this to say:

As immigrant artists for whom so much has been sacrificed, so many dreams have been deferred, we already doubt so much. It might have been simpler, safer to become the more helpful doctors, lawyers, engineers our parents wanted us to be. When our worlds are literally crumbling, we tell ourselves how right they may have been, our elders, about our passive careers as distant witnesses. Who do we think we are? We think we are people who risked not existing at all. People who might have been killed, either by a government or by nature, even before we were born. Some of us think we are accidents of literacy. I do. We think we are people who might not have been able to go to school at all, who might never have learned to read or write. We think we are the children of people who have lived in the shadows for too long. (19)

Clearly, such a declaration could not have emanated identically from Alvarez; the differences in their biographies suggest that Alvarez (nor figures like the Henríquez siblings, nor their parents) was nowhere near the kind of "accident of literacy" that someone like Danticat can convincingly claim to be.[5] But Danticat's terminology here does in some ways help us to understand a larger discursive, institutional, and historical process that might fold into its analysis the instance of an Alvarez as well; we can thus begin to ask here to what extent a fuller analysis of the "accidental" logic of so much coming-to-literacy in our world might help us to recondition, rather than, say, recuperate, our critical sense of the possible relationships that such accidents of literacy might take to what Terry Eagleton has termed the "event" (or perhaps an event-status more broadly construed?) of "literature." This alternatively tense dialectic, at once ontological and historical, between the accident and the event, may help us to think through more rigorously, and more productively, alternative relations linking literary to epistemological to political projects, especially as alternatives to important and still-influential analyses like Beverley's from twenty years ago.

We can conclude this section of our discussion with a brief passage near the end of Danticat's *Brother, I'm Dying*, where she recalls a story she heard from her uncle about his most vivid memory of life in Haiti during the same period of imperial occupation that Alvarez explores late in *Salomé*. In the last years of the US occupation of Haiti, Danticat tells us, her grandparents kept their children away from the violent threat of the occupying Marines by forbidding their straying far from their mountain village home to the larger towns in the valley below where US Marines were stationed. Once, however, they had no choice but to send their oldest son to market in one of those towns. Danticat writes:

When my uncle finally reached the marketplace at midday, after hours and hours of walking, he saw a group of young white men in dark high boots and khakis at its bamboo-fenced entrance. There were perhaps six or seven of them, and they seemed to be kicking something on the ground. My uncle had never seen white men before, and their pink, pale skins gave some credence to his mother's notion that white people had *po lanvè*, skins turned inside out, so that if they didn't wear heavy clothing, you might always be looking at their insides ... the[se] white men seemed to him to be quite agitated. Were they laughing? Screaming in another language? They kept kicking the thing on the ground as though it were a soccer ball, bouncing it to one another with the rounded tips of their boots. Taking small careful steps to remain the same distance away as the other bystanders, my uncle finally saw what it was: a man's head, ... full of black peppercorn hair[,] Blood ... dripping out of the severed neck, forming dusty dark red bubbles in the dirt. (246–247)

How to "read" such a passage, written, and presented, to us, its readers, in a text that signals its generic operation as that of literary memoir, one where the horrific incident depicted exists, if it happened at all, at a distance of removal not only measurable in both geographical and chronological terms, but also in terms of the degrees of reportage and communication separating the witness Joseph from his interlocutor niece, Edwidge, from the author, Danticat, to her readers, us, here, now? At further remove still is the account of Joseph's mother, Edwidge's grandmother, offering her son a tool for handling the encounter between black Haitians and their white American occupiers via the figurative characterization in Kreyòl of white people having inverted skins, where that invocation of inversion seems to both promise access (however violent) to the interiority of those occupiers and at the same time name the rhetorical function of the passage itself, as it inverts readerly expectations that the object being kicked around by the American Marines might actually be a soccer ball rather than a man's severed head. One way of course to understand the question, "how to 'read' such a passage?" might be to translate it as, "how to 'describe' what happens" in it, and at whatever level one might want to claim for the occurrence the status of (literary, historical) event. There would in turn be more than one answer to such a question, but the one we can offer here might be something like: a change in our critical understanding of the work of Haitian (Hispaniolan-, Caribbean-, Latinx-) Diasporic literature, especially in its commitment to retrieving alongside and in concert with history, a sense of the actual past as necessarily mediated beyond recording, and even mimesis, and through narration, and figuration, and invention.

Work clearly remains to be done in literary and cultural studies as we attempt to account for the historical emergence of a body of expressive material by writers of, for example, the US-Latinx-Hispaniolan-Caribbean diaspora, and in ways that do not proceed from ready-made decisions about that larger literary project's likely relationship to any set of potentially relevant, and stubbornly hegemonic, national-imperial or -state projects. The contemporary literary space, like the contemporary political space, insists on too heterogeneous, uneven, and nonidentical a relationship with anything that might still want to insist on the presumptively dominant authority of the classical national state for the conventional critique "against" literature to hold. Literature, like history, in history, and, in critical, complex ways, *as* history, continues to have everything to tell us about the complex conditions of a cultural and political modernity primarily attentive to the violent logics, and the urgent demands, of occupation, diaspora and empire, and beyond these, of quite collective formations of kinship, and memory, and survival, and desire, and even love.

NOTES

1. Beverley helped to establish and influence the anti-literature, pro-testimonio, then post-testimonio moves in Latin American literary/cultural/subaltern/indigenous/post-dictatorship studies across work like *Against Literature* (University of Minnesota Press, 1993), the essays collected in the *Testimonio: On the Politics of Truth* volume (University of Minnesota Press, 2004) and *Latinamericanism After 9/11* (Duke UP, 2011). Other representative projects in this movement (among many others) include Idelber Avelar's *The Untimely Present: Post-dictatorial Latin American Fiction and the Task of Mourning* (Duke UP, 1999); Alberto Moreiras's *The Exhaustion of Difference: The Politics of Latin American Cultural Studies* (Duke UP, 2001); Arturo Arias, Ed.'s *The Rigoberta Menchú Controversy* (University of Minnesota Press, 2001); Brett Levinson's *The Ends of Literature: The Latin American "Boom" in the Neoliberal Marketplace* (Stanford UP, 2001); both Jean Franco's *The Decline and Fall of the Lettered City: Latin America in the Cold War* (Harvard UP, 2002) and *Cruel Modernity* (Duke UP, 2013); Ileana Rodríguez's *Liberalism at Its Limits: Crime and Terror in the Latin American Cultural Text* (University of Pittsburgh Press, 2009), and finally the text that will represent this essay's own convergence with this genealogy in our last section, Horacio Legrás's *Literature and Subjection: The Economy of Writing and Marginality in Latin America* (University of Pittsburgh Press, 2008).

2. Beverley's focus here on literature's function in mostly twentieth century Latin American contexts as ideological state apparatus, as simultaneously the curation of an official national canon and an effective instrument in public education, anticipates from a different angle similar concerns articulated in the passage by Jean-Marie Schaeffer discussed in note 9 in Chapter 7 below, admittedly from an essay about literary studies and literary education in France.

3. Danticat herself in the "Create Dangerously" essay articulates her own account of literature's historical work, perhaps its historical task, in terms that strikingly echo Trouillot's: "The immigrant artist," she argues, "shares with all other artists the desire to interpret and possibly remake his or her own world. So though we may not be creating as dangerously as our forebears,—though we are not risking torture, beatings, execution, though exile does not threaten us into perpetual silence,—still, while we work bodies are littering the streets somewhere. People are buried under rubble somewhere. Survivors are living in makeshift tent cities and refugee camps somewhere, shielding their heads from rain, closing their eyes, covering their ears, to shout out the sounds of military 'aid' helicopters. And still, many are reading, and writing, quietly, quietly" (18).

4. In a longer version of this project, I would turn beyond this early scene in a narrative that traces its protagonist's life backward toward her youth to the chapters devoted to Camila's life as a young woman, chapters that coincide with the US occupation of the Dominican Republic in the nineteen teens and early twenties; these chapters also coincide with the Camila's early explorations of her lesbian desire, the evolution of her relationship with her older brother Pedro, and her ongoing negotiation of the legacy of her already-legendary mother, Salomé. As a friendly rejoinder to Beverley's invocation of Pedro Henríquez in his analysis of twentieth century Latin American literature and literary studies and their relevant ties to the hegemonic work of the national state, I would want to offer Alvarez's strategic reimaging of Pedro's own early life through the lens of his sister Camila. As two prominent participants in the literary and cultural labor of a population that Beverley might want still to class as a "national-bourgeois intelligentsia," it matters here vitally, in ways that Alvarez's work makes clear strictly at the level of biographical fact before any fictionalizing, literary embellishment, that brother and sister Henríquez did most of their work in exile, in the US (significantly, at the University of Minnesota, Harvard University, and Vassar and Middlebury Colleges), in Cuba, in Mexico, and in additional countries for the more itinerant Pedro, and therefore that work like theirs may on the one hand bear the strong if complex traces of a nationalist hegemonic project, but on the other the more insistent conditions of that work's emergence remain occupation,

displacement, and exile. "The production of traces," is always, indeed, "the production of silences."

5. Danticat's strategic turn here to the precarious, provisional, indeed accidental, occurrence of her own basic literacy productively opens this discussion out toward another important recent thread in Latin American literary and cultural studies, exemplified by Abraham Acosta's deconstruction of subaltern subjects' conventional relationships to illiteracy and orality, specifically by opening up the possible conceptualizations of the former category. "By illiteracy," Acosta argues, "I do not mean just the inability to read and write, nor am I appealing to the voice's primacy over writing; illiteracy as I am developing it should not be confused with the characteristic—individual or cultural—defined by a lack or deficiency of lettered culture and practices. Illiteracy is not the property, characteristic, or identity of those who cannot read. Rather I use the term to express the condition of semiological excess and ungovernability that emerges from the critical disruption of the field of intelligibility within which traditional and resistant modes of reading are defined and positioned. Illiteracy is not a thing nor in itself an object of study but rather an unconcealment." See Acosta, Abraham, *Thresholds of Illiteracy: Theory, Latin American and the Crisis of Resistance* (New York, NY: Fordham UP, 2014): 9. One might understand the present discussion as an attempt to identify what might remain "illiterate," that is, semiologically "excessive," and "ungovernable," about Latinx literary studies today, as it continues to struggle to articulate what exactly it does, and why exactly it does it.

CHAPTER 5

The Testimonial Imagination or, Literary Practice "After" Testimonio

Abstract "The Testimonial Imagination" extends the discussion of Beverley and testimonio launched in the previous section to include two additional, and quite central texts of the Latin American literary tradition, Rigoberta Menchú's testimonio, and Reinaldo Arenas' memoir, *Before Night Falls*. While this section also discusses work by the Cuban-American novelist Cristina García, it shifts the geographical orientation of the larger discussion away from the Caribbean and toward Central America, specifically Guatemala, in order to trouble as well the conventional regional logics of Latinx literary studies by bringing the archipelago into more direct conversation with the isthmus.

Keywords Indigeneity · Queerness · Cold War · Revolution · Exile · Genocide

This section extends the preceding discussion by pairing two seemingly disparate comments, one a fairly thrown away aside in a piece of gossipy political analysis by John Beverley, the other a bit more pointed a corollary conclusion to an immigration policy decision announced by President Barack Obama on the verge of leaving office. The first is from the "Preface" of Beverley's 2004 book, *Testimonio: On the Politics of Truth*, and it comes up at the end of this longish passage:

© The Author(s) 2019
R. L. Ortiz, *Latinx Literature Now*, Literatures of the Americas,
https://doi.org/10.1007/978-3-030-04708-5_5

Generally speaking, protagonists of *testimonio* in the Cold War years, like myself, saw it as a narrative form linked closely to national liberation movements and other social struggles inspired by Marxism. By contrast, the skeptics or antagonists of *testimonio* (some of them former leftists) often resorted to a kind of "red-baiting"—the McCarthyite tactic of disqualifying someone else's ideas by the allegation that he or she was a Communist or sympathetic to Communism—unless, of course, the particular *testimonio* in question, say, Solzhenitsyn's *Gulag Archipelago* or Reinaldo Arenas's *Before Night Falls*, fit their ideological agenda, in which case it was true and compelling. (JB, x)

Anyone familiar with the production, circulation, and reception histories of testimonio will immediately find certain aspects of this statement striking: first, there is the sense of significant historical distance between the moment of this passage's utterance in 2004 and the "Cold War years," already more than a decade gone, which had conditioned the life of testimonio when it first emerged and enjoyed its early political and critical consolidations primarily around indigenous Guatemalan activist Rigoberta Menchú's 1982 telling of her life story; second, and perhaps more relevant for the patient readers of this essay, is the recourse to the dynamics of protagonism and antagonism that drive Beverley's rhetoric here in describing the dialectically, presumably ideologically, polar critical responses to testimonio generally, but certainly specifically to Menchú's; and finally there is that rather thrownaway reference at the end to what Beverley seems to consider examples of testimonio that would better suit the ideological demands of more conservative, anti-left or anti-Communist readers and critics, specifically Aleksander Solzhenitsyn's account of his captivity and torture in the Soviet Gulag, and Reinaldo Arenas's memoir of his life in Cuba before and after the 1959 Revolution, and in the United States after Mariel and during the AIDS crisis of the 1980s that eventually precipitated his suicide in 1990. This first comment thus offers a couple of important points for this discussion to take up: one is that a critic with the intellectual authority about testimonio that Beverley clearly wielded at the time seems to admit here that *Before Night Falls* actually qualifies as testimonio; the second is that, were that the case, we might potentially learn something valuable from a staged critical encounter between Menchú and Arenas, as each in their own way protagonists of testimonio, an encounter that has yet to be staged in any meaningful way (as far as I can discern) by anyone in the larger critical and scholarly establishment in or across either the fields of Latin American or US Latinx literary studies.

The second, more pointed, comment comes from President Barack Obama while announcing the end of the 1995, Clinton-era "wet-foot, dry-foot" policy governing Cuban immigration to the United States; "By taking this step," Obama observed, "we are treating Cuban migrants the same way we treat migrants from other countries." In the January 12, 2017 *New York Times* report entitled "Obama Ends Exemptions for Cubans Who Arrive Without Visas," the *Times* reporters also quote then-DHS Secretary Jeh Johnson as saying, "the past is past, the future will be different," and Peter Kornbluh of the National Security Archive's Cuba Documentation Project as saying that the logic of Cuban "exceptionalism" in US immigration policy was "a relic of the Cold War." In light of the well-documented surge in undocumented Cuban migration (in the many tens of thousands) to the United States since the announcement of the thaw in US–Cuba relations on December 17, 2014, a surge that in particular saw dramatic increases in Cubans trying to reach the United States not across the Straits of Florida but over land, north through Central America to the US–Mexico border, and in light of this migrant stream's merging into the larger flow of desperate humanity making its way northward from Central America, including from Guatemala, to the United States, this feels, for better or worse, like an important opportunity to re-think some of the prevailing and indeed perpetual "antagonisms," some of them recalcitrant "relics" of a Cold War now a quarter century in the past, that traditionally pitted Cuba "against" the United States geopolitically on the one hand, but also, sadly, pitted Cuban immigrants to the US "against" their fellow migrants from other Latin and Central American countries, migrants who, especially in recent years, have a strong case to make in favor of refugee status given the extreme forms of violent criminal and political persecution they face in countries like Guatemala.

If in the 2004 Beverley quote we already hear a relaxation of the dominant dialectical tensions governing political, social and even intellectual life in the Cold War years, there figured in the salient opposition between communism and capitalism, an opposition metonymized in Beverley's discussion in the tension between ideologically distinct instantiations of testimonio, in the 2017 Obama quote (and in the echoes from Johnson and Kornbluh) we hear some final dissolution of that most stubborn vestige of Cold War geopolitical logic, the exceptionalism of a Cuba that seemed more mired in that dialectical logic a quarter century past its resolution (for better or worse) everywhere else in the world (including the rest of Latin America) than in the immediate historical realities all around it, in particular the increasingly fluid, and volatile, shifts in political, economic and social conditions driving the movement of bodies across borders not only between Cuba and the United States, but in the larger regional spaces of the Caribbean, Central America, and Mexico.

I therefore want to take the occasion of these current conditions, and this present discussion, to think our way beyond the "perpetual antagonism" that has for so long governed both US–Cuba historical relations and their various forms of study and reflection by complicating some of the dialectical logics and tensions I've just put into play here. I'll start by returning to John Beverley to mark how his provisional, almost ersatz invocation of Arenas (who never comes up again in Beverley's book) opens up the possibility of a way out of the unresolvable dialectics of east-west/north-south/right-left inherited from the Cold War, and lingering so far beyond its demise, via a "trialectic" configuration that, in this case, complicates left-testimonio v. right-testimonio tensions (and beyond them, for Beverley, the larger tensions pitting testimonio "against" literature itself), by reading Menchú and Arenas together, and having each disturb and disrupt the dialectical stalemate that still governs the critical reception of the other. And while I will not have occasion to return to the question of the "wet-foot, dry-foot" policy here, I do want to mark how former President Obama's observation regarding the end of Cuban exceptionalism in US policy parallels this kind of triangulating disruption of a formerly dialectical stalemate: treating Cubans "the way we treat migrants from other countries" not only opens up a geopolitical vista that formerly only saw Cuba in relation to the United States, or in contrast to all "other countries," but also opens up the possibility of seeing Cuba, for the first time meaningfully *alongside* those other countries, and, in contemporary contexts, perhaps most importantly El Salvador, Honduras, and Guatemala. Given the central encounter I want to stage here between Arenas and Menchú, the key national "trialectic" driving the rest of the discussion in this section will use Guatemala to stand in for the rest of Central America, and in particular post-Cold War, post-civil-war Central America, and allow it to work as the "third" term in a dynamic that also wants to imagine, finally, a set of post-Cold War US–Cuba relations no longer held frozen in time, again, by a hopelessly posthumous historical and political dialectic. But to pose Guatemala as the third term here is not to render it secondary to that dialectic: indeed, in the larger space of this analysis Cuba can also be said to pose as the "third" term in a competing dialectic between Guatemala and the United States, and the United States itself can enter from another angle to disrupt the one tying Cuba to Guatemala.

This discussion can only cursorily gesture toward the rich history of testimonio criticism that has orbited around Menchú's text, and primarily in relation to both Beverley's critical sponsorship of it since the 1980s and the revelations (thanks to David Stoll) of its failures of veracity that started to plague it in the 1990s, leading to the kind of critical distancing from it that we see in Beverley's work from 2004. Even post-Stoll, and in part because of the controversy, the testimonio has enjoyed a long and remarkably sustained critical afterlife, from the collection examining the *Rigoberta Menchú Controversy* edited by Arturo Arias and an important chapter on "The Aura of Testimonio" in Alberto Moreiras's *The Exhaustion of Difference* (both from 2001) to equally important interventions (mostly chapters in books) into the critical debate around it by such influential critics as Doris Sommer (1999), Brett Levinson (2002), Maria Josefina Saldaña Portillo (2003), and more recently Abraham Acosta (2014). Arenas too has obviously enjoyed a robust critical afterlife, one that certainly extends past his tragic death in 1990 to today, and along the way collects important critical work by scholars including Francisco Soto (1990), two books by Rafael Ocasio (2003 and 2007), and more recent work by Wendy-Jayne McMahon (2012) and Jorge Olivares (2013). In addition, both Menchú and Arenas have been the subjects of cinematic works, he in the 1984 Nestor Almendros documentary *Improper Conduct* as well as in Julian Schnabel's 2000 feature adaptation of *Before Night Falls*, she in a pair of documentaries by Pamela Yates, *When the Mountains Tremble* (1983) and *Granito* (2011). In addition, we can also briefly note here the parallel failures of veracity in both her testimonio and his, how those failures, far from fatal, open up the far richer analysis (based on all the extant scholarship cited here) of the status and function of the discursive field, and of literature and its others, during and beyond the Cold War, and across regional and hemispheric circuits that refuse the old and waning geographically conventional logics of Latin Americanist as well as US Latinx-ist critical and cultural reflection.

It also bears reflecting briefly here on the striking biographical parallels uniting Arenas and Menchú, from their mutual births into abject rural poverty, to their immersion in the local ways of life of their communities as children, their uneven and never guaranteed access to education, especially to literacy, to their eventual migrations to their respective national capitals to experience firsthand the rising tides of revolutionary forces that would transform each of them politically in distinct but incommensurable ways, to their almost symmetrical experiences of political persecution (his taking the form of his own prolonged censorship, legal betrayal, incarceration, and abuse; hers taking some of those forms but also the extreme force of murderous violence inflicted on members of her family and her people), even to the manner in which, during periods of exile (hers in Paris, his in New York), they performed their testimonial work first orally for recording by tape before the transcription of those oral accounts into print for publication. Such a reflection should also, of course, take into account the failures of some parallels: she was younger than he by some sixteen years; in the dialectical political logics of the Cold War they (presumably) landed on opposing sides; her extreme abjection as political target was anchored primarily in her status as a member of the indigenous Maya-Quiché people (with all the accompanying forms of corollary abjection), his initially in his family's poverty, but eventually most violently in his status as queer, which targeted him for political persecution in Cuba, and rendered him radically vulnerable to illness and death due to the AIDS epidemic ravaging Reagan-era New York City; she devoted much of her political life to movements in which she eventually took prominent leadership roles while he turned his political activism increasingly toward his writing, only emerging as a compellingly public symbolic figure in both queer and Cuban-exile politics after his death and the publication of his memoir (first in Spanish, then English) in the early 1990s; and finally, she lives on, still politically active in a Guatemala that continues to reel from both direct and indirect aftermaths of the long-past civil war and Cold War geopolitics, while he is long passed away, more than a quarter century gone (like the Cold War itself) and persisting only in the documentary, creative, critical, and scholarly archive in which this current discussion hopes to play a productive part.

For what remains of this discussion I will introduce and describe what I take to be a still-occluded item in that archive, *The Lady Matador's Hotel*, a novel published in 2010 by the Cuban–American writer Cristina

García. It wasn't widely known until recently that Garcia's father was born in Guatemala (though his family moved to Cuba when he was a child and he identified as Cuban), but *Lady Matador* extends what I call a post-Cuban geographical opening, in Garcia's novelistic work after her first two novels, *Dreaming in Cuban* (1992) and *The Agüero Sisters* (1997), toward Central America, and specifically toward post-civil war Guatemala. This geographical opening begins with the episodes set in China and Vietnam in 2003s *Monkey Hunting* (which admittedly is still mostly set in Cuba), but that extends in 2007s *A Handbook to Luck* to a primary setting in diasporic 1990s Los Angeles, where Cuban, Iranian, Salvadoran, and Korean characters meet and interact while multiple flashbacks take us back in time to their respective homelands during the Cold War, and finally, in 2010s *Lady Matador*, lands in an unnamed Central American capital, a "tropical capital with blue-black volcanoes" that appear as one character lands there on a plane (22), this city for that reason cannot be San Salvador, or Tegucigalpa, or Managua, leaving only Guatemala City as the possible referent for it. Into this setting Garcia introduces a sextet of characters, three natives and three visitors, but only two of whom will interest us here: one is a young woman, Aura Estrada, whom Garcia depicts as a native of the country, and a former *guerrillera* in the struggle against the military junta that held her people in its murderous, genocidal grip for the length of a bloody civil war some years in the past; the other is Ricardo Morán, a Cuban-exile poet, a Marielito and now a New Yorker, who is visiting the unnamed capital with his wife as they attempt the foreign adoption of a local baby to save their troubled marriage. I don't in this discussion mean to overstate how much either Aura is modeled on Rigoberta or Ricardo is on Reinaldo; Garcia is too subtle an artist to treat such characterizations so heavy-handedly, especially when she's clearly interested in asserting a historical grounding for her imagined world that might implicate both of them. So the differences here matter as much as the similarities: Aura, while active in the armed struggle, doesn't rise to a leadership role, lending her enough anonymity that she can remain and work in the capital in the years following the truce and end of the civil war; Ricardo, for starters, isn't queer, and his exploits in the capital, as he negotiates both his troubled marriage by flirting with women other than his wife and his discovery of fatherhood through the love that flourishes in him for his adopted infant daughter, offer a quite different alchemy of sexual affect, artistry, and politics than the kind we get from Arenas.

But if differences matter so do the striking similarities. Like Menchú, Aura's backstory includes the almost total extermination of her family, and especially the notable manner of her brother's murder. As García's narrator tells us in an early scene:

> Aura rarely prays, but when she does it's to her beloved dead: to Papi, who passed away when she was ten of a blood disease the curanderas couldn't heal; to her brother, Julio, set aflame by a sadistic army patrol while defending the family's cornfield, to Mamá, who, after helplessly witnessing her son's death, stopped eating and sleeping until her soul joined his; to Aura's lover Juan Carlos, blown apart by a landmine … If she begins to tally the savagery, she wouldn't stop. (7)

Julio's is the ghost who mostly haunts Aura through the narrative, so it matters that of all her dead he is the one most closely linked to Menchú's biography; anyone familiar with the testimonio and the controversy surrounding it will know that Menchú's teenage brother Petrocinio was set aflame by a government death squad, and that her account of that event was faulty in that she was actually not present when it occurred, though in the testimonio she implies she was. García here also seems to deflect some of that ethical complexity onto her depiction of Aura's mother, emphasizing the "helplessness" of "witnessing" such extreme atrocities; Menchú, ironically, wasn't lying about the manner of her brother's murder, only in the way she tried to position herself as the direct witness to an event she didn't actually see. In this way, Petrocinio, in his death, "haunted" Rigoberta too, and one has to ask what García might have meant to accomplish in dramatizing this dynamic in such an approximate yet compelling way as she absorbs elements of Menchú's testimonial truth, and testimonial lies, into the fully fictional, and committedly historical, world of her novel?

A longer version of this discussion might also pursue the choice to name her counter-Rigoberta "Aura": has Garcia read Moreiras' chapter on the "Aura of Testimonio"? If so, how is she responding to the analysis Moreiras offers there in part of the fetishistic tendency of some testimonio criticism to relegate Menchú's indigeneity to some inaccessible space of an authentic Real? "Aura" in the genealogy of critical theory that Moreiras represents originates with the Benjaminian analysis of the lost "aura" of the work of art in the age of mechanical reproduction; as

such, it bears structural similarities to the Freudian concept of the fet-
ish, but also of the uncanny (see the next section). If Garcia hadn't read
Moreiras, and had instead herself arrived at the notion that a character
like her Aura might be vulnerable to a similar kind of fetishization, one
that links her indigeneity and subaltern existence to a lost or inaccessible Real that demands (impossible) restitution, especially for the sort of
critical reflection that desperately wants to recover an authenticity and a
fullness of being it can only ever mourn from its alienated perch in the
webwork of discourse, then in what ways might we consider García's
strategy of naming here something other than unintentional coincidence,
in what ways, indeed, might it present itself as uncanny?

Ricardo Morán too shares some important approximate similarities
with his double, Reinaldo Arenas. In one scene, García has him watching
televised reports of elections in the unnamed country that is and isn't
Guatemala, and he begins to compose some verse, but then thinks twice:

> We are the news/We are the light, the poet scribbles in his pocket note-
> book, then crosses it out. It sounds like a bad political slogan, something
> El Comandante might have dreamed up. Ricardo detested the Cuban
> Revolution's distortions, the magnetism of its crass, one-size-fits-all prop-
> aganda. During his last year in Havana, everyone communicated through
> subtext and his friends resorted to writing science fiction to fool the cen-
> sors. He could spend the rest of the day cataloguing the ruins. (26)

This passage sounds like something that, with minor revisions, could
have been lifted out of *Before Night Falls*. Other passages in García's
novel offer additional parallels to Arenas' life, including a reference to
Ricardo's own political imprisonment "as an undesirable" (177).

But here I'll let those parallels stand and turn instead in closing this
section to the ones that run between Ricardo, García's alter-Arenas, and
Aura, her alter-Menchú. In the passages just quoted, each character is
not only positioned as a direct survivor of an abusive totalitarian political
regime and its most murderous practices, each is also positioned as an
explicitly testimonial subject, a chronicler of carnage at the hands of the
state. As Aura imagines herself "tallying the savagery" and Ricardo imagines himself "cataloguing the ruins," we can imagine both of them, as
they're imagined together by García, collecting into themselves, and into
her narrative, direct lines of testimonial force from the real (living and

dead) chroniclers they recall, and invoke. At the novel's end, García imagines each of these two characters meeting on a bus headed north after each commits a crime: she's killed a murderous colonel, he's kidnapped a child. We get the scene from Aura's perspective:

> There are others on the bus with her, all asleep except for the Cuban poet with the swaddled infant two rows back ... He hasn't stopped whispering, either to himself or the baby, she isn't sure which. Aura ... suspects he's reciting verse, overhears the phrase: *the lime tree's agitated shade*. He must be a fugitive, like her. (201–202)

The line Aura overhears Ricardo reciting actually belongs to the modernist poet Anna Akhmatova, who lived out her life in Soviet Russia, and who committed her work (like the book *Requiem* where the line appears) to witnessing the worst abuses of her country's government. This closing image, therefore, returns us to where this section started, where we heard John Beverley sum up a now bygone but then world-shaping political divide by reducing it to a set of competing readerly preferences for one kind of testimonio or another, depending on a text's origins either in Russia, or Cuba, or Guatemala. But it also returns us to Barack Obama's equating of Cuban immigrants, from now on, with "migrants from other countries": "He must be a fugitive," García has Aura observe, "just like her."

This section can thus conclude by asking: given that García wrote this almost a decade ago, at the beginning of what we can now call the bygone "Obama era," and during an early phase in a process of violent human displacement in the Americas that, all the current and notorious declarations of its possible cessation notwithstanding, shows no signs of abating, what should we make of what feels like an uncanny historical prediction, on García's part, when she imagines these two "fugitive" migrants, one Cuban, one Guatemalan, making their way to a "north" we might assume we could spot on a map, though García never takes us *there*. Instead she leaves us, as I'll leave this, in an imagined place within an imagined place, a place in fiction, and in literature, far from history in one respect while absolutely within it in another, and far from all the testimonial forms of its remembering, a place that García imagines Aura imagining thus: "She pictures an encampment of spirits murmuring in the desert, negotiating in the afterlife what they couldn't settle alive" (202).

CHAPTER 6

Un-Homey States:
Econo-Mimetics of Homelessness
in US Latinx Poetry

Abstract "Un-Homey States" uses Freud's influential elaboration of the concept of the uncanny to address questions of citizenship, authorized and unauthorized immigration, and forms of radical, often violent depatriation and practical, existential homelessness, all of compelling, urgent interest over recent decades to US Latinx studies writ large; the section then deploys Freud's concept to read closely works of lyrical verse by a trio of Chicanx poets, Eduardo Corral, Rigoberto González, and Ada Limón, who have published important collections in the second decade of the twenty-first century, a period conditioned simultaneously by state failures precipitating from both the financial collapse of 2008 and the indefinite stalemate on comprehensive immigration reform in the United States.

Keywords Uncanny · Poetry · Immigration · Undocumented · Homeless · Family · Domesticity · Mobility

I open this section with Freud's century-old and overworked 1919 essay "The Uncanny," and the dated and overworked concept it elaborates, primarily because I still find in the original untranslated essay's reliance on German terms rooted in concepts of "home," the homey and homely (and their opposites), a potent resource for analyzing even very contemporary representations of traumatic and uncanny experience that can ground us in an indisputably material and historical reality exceedingly productive of both trauma and anxious, fearful disorientation, and simultaneously grant us license to proceed with our analysis of that reality by way of committed aesthetic practices with varying relationships to representational realism and its countless imagined others. "Home" here can start with the mere question of housing, of who enjoys the guarantee of shelter and who doesn't, of how the struggle to secure and maintain shelter that isn't ever guaranteed requires of those who can manage it the commitment of time to secure space, the expenditure of at least short-term but also long-term labor and, for some, long-term debt, and for those who can't manage it the dependence on others, from the family, to the community, to the state, to offer it; "home" also invokes its material opposite, which is not the (un)home of (un)homely, but the absence or failure or refusal of "home" denoted in "homeless," the state of living primarily without shelter, which is certainly a more basic and debilitating privation than living without a house, or even a home. Beyond this invocation of the actual material political economy of literal housing and shelter, we can also hear in the negative semantics that both "un"and "less" visit on the concept and experience of "home" something of the failure of a conventional, classical and traditional concept of the nation as homeland, another set of critical and compelling failures in our contemporary moment: national states and national economies increasingly fail to protect let alone secure and sustain national populations, forcing subpopulations of their nationals to migrate in mass numbers, sometimes with but often without authorization, and as often to escape political violence either at the hands of those very states or as a result of their failures as states, while more stable and open states stumble over themselves to side with either pole of the contemporary geopolitical dialectic, a dialectic pitting "open," neoliberal transnational globalization against a retrenching, protectionist, nativist nationalism, and neither the friend, if sometimes the host, of the most vulnerably homeless among us, those of us caught in the currents of a system of mass global dislodgement that shows no signs of receding or abating. These failures on the part of national states and national economies, generated and sustained as they are by that increasingly anti-national global system, leave in their wake, and grind into the bodies and souls of the masses of the economically and politically displaced, the question of what happens to culture, especially but not only national culture, and of what culture (national, transnational, regional, or local) can make happen in the face of the shock waves of collective experience that characterize this general historical moment, and challenge any and all attempts at representational, critical or creative, capture.

There are two relevant takeaways from Freud's essay to consider as we embark into this section of the larger discussion.[1] One has to do with the amount of time and space and effort Freud famously devotes to a kind of semantic excavation of the word and a logical excavation of the concept early in the essay. After he introduces the German near-synonyms "*heimlich* ['homely']" and "*heimisch* ['native']" and begins to deconstruct the conventional logic of opposition that would usually govern how these nouns absorb the inverting violence of the "un-" that smashes through the familiar to the foreign, that renders the *heimlich unheimlich*, Freud takes a detour through a series of spatial openings, of openings toward spatiality, that we should notice here. Following Jentsch, who "ascribes the essential factor in the production of the feeling of uncanniness to intellectual uncertainty," Freud restates this formulation in spatial terms: "the uncanny would always, as it were, be something one does not know one's way about in. The better orientated in his environment a person is," Freud goes on, "the less readily he will get the impression of something uncanny in regard to objects and events in it" (221). Freud explicitly signals that he finds Jentsch's formulation "incomplete," but that does little to disqualify his spatial turn to experiences of "orientation" and "environment" to elaborate that formulation. Immediately following this passage Freud detours further, into the territory of what he calls "other languages," but finding little there that is helpful, observing that dictionaries in those languages (among them Latin and Greek, Arabic and Hebrew, as well as English, Spanish, French, Italian, and Portuguese) "tell us nothing new, perhaps only because we ourselves speak a language that is foreign" (221). Memorable among the synonyms and cognates he cites from these dictionaries are: ξένος from the Greek; *locus suspectus* and *intempesta nocte* from the Latin; *ghastly* and *haunted* from English; and *sospechoso, siniestro* from Spanish. Two additional corollary points to keep in mind from this first takeaway: the way *heimlich* already contains "*unheimlich*" qualities, when the familiar becomes the private, hence the secret and the hidden and unsettling; the difference between the return of "surmounted" superstitions of a society's primitive past and the triggering of otherwise successfully repressed infantile complexes.

The second takeaway comes much later in the essay, but like the passage just discussed hinges on a metaphorical use of the spatial, here in the guises of "the realm of fiction" (247), and the "more fertile province" that Freud takes "*literature*" to be, in the latter's distinct capacity for depictions of uncanny experience that exceed and intensify what's available from merely "direct" experience (249). We should therefore "differentiate," he concludes, "between the uncanny that we actually experience and the uncanny that we merely picture or read about" (247). Uncannily, some paragraphs later Freud himself appears to rethink the dismissive "merely" that modifies the activities of "picturing" and "reading" that exemplify two of the practices that might situate us in that "realm" of the fictive, the literary, indeed the aesthetic, if one were to name the largest of the discursive, conceptual, and experiential spaces to which his elaboration of the uncanny anchors us. "Picturing" and "reading" merely spin for Freud here in the mode of passive engagement of the aesthetic, naming what audiences do; but by the time he plunges most directly into his discussion of the literary uncanny, his focus turns quite decidedly to the active work of the writer/artist in characterizing literature (or art's) more "fertile" production of uncanny effects. "[L]iterature," Freud argues, "is a much more fertile province than the uncanny in real life, for it contains the whole of the latter and something more besides, something that cannot be found in real life" (249). This discussion of the uncanny in art takes up the entire final section of Freud's essay, and while it makes numerous important observations about the psychic dynamics that go into the production of such uncanny effects, I'm more interested for the purposes of this discussion in the drama Freud weaves into this passage of the creative act itself, of the active performative practice of the writer/artist as both productive creation of a thing and a moment (an object-event or event-object) in and as the text and/or artwork, and also as an assertive soliciting address of an audience.

Across these concluding passages of the essay Freud stages the drama thus: first, he tells us that "the imaginative writer has this licence among many others, that he can select his world of representation so that it coincides with the realities with which we are familiar or departs from them in what particulars he pleases. We [for our part as readers] accept his ruling in every case." This power of selection will determine whether and to what degree our experience of the artwork will result in any uncanny effects, and ironically the likelihood of their occurring diminishes as the degree of magic, supernaturalism or fantasy driving the artwork increases. "The situation," Freud argues:

is altered as soon as the writer pretends to move in the world of common reality. In this case he accepts as well all the conditions operating to
produce uncanny feelings in real life; and everything that would have an
uncanny effect in reality is in his story. But in this case he can even increase
his effect and multiply it far beyond what could happen in reality, by bringing about events which never or very rarely happen in fact. In doing this
he is in a sense betraying us to the superstitiousness which we have osten-
sibly surmounted; he deceives us by promising to give us the sober truth,
and then after all overstepping it. We react to his inventions as we would
have reacted to real experiences; by the time we have seen through his trick
it is already too late and the author has achieved his object. (250–251)

I'm interested, as I close this exposition of Freud, in the complex inter-
active and transactional model of artist/audience engagement that he
dramatizes in this passage; on the one hand, there seems to be an almost
contractual understanding here between the two parties that set the
terms of the breach occurring when the artist "betrays" his audience by
introducing elements into his art world that in turn "betray" the realist terms upon which that world seemed to be conditioned; on another
hand, this contractual logic suggests a more imbedded ethical tension,
where the artistic betrayal seems aimed at the audience's clearly mis-
placed trust in, perhaps even loyalty to, the integrity of the artist's inten-
tions; on yet a third hand, the confession to an unwanted deception here
seems to take us to an even deeper space of intimacy, of complex manip-
ulation and negotiation that ambiguates any conventional expectations,
especially of pleasure and pain, of placid certainty and anxious doubt, on
the part of the audience, and in a manner that takes what appears still to
be a primarily aesthetic encounter and teases it (and us) toward the space
of the erotic. "[T]he storyteller," Freud concludes, "has a peculiarly
directive power over us; by means of the moods he can put us into, he
is able to guide the current of our emotions, to dam it up in one direction and make it flow in another, and he often obtains a great variety of
effects from the same material" (251).

   The current discussion makes no pretense at offering cultural, creative, literary practice as either therapeutic or redemptive in the face of the
violent material and historical shocks inventoried in the introduction to
this section. If anything, it merely takes some cues from Freud's analysis
of how the uncanny can (still!) productively travel from actual experience

into the fictive registers of the aesthetic, if only to deepen and intensify our encounters with difficulty, anxiety, ambiguity, and even violence, and in a space that, while "safer," offers nothing like complete safety from the modes of threat, and risk, and danger that should haunt our collective imaginations as much as they haunt our actual lives. In what remains of this section, I want to touch on some literary work that flirts with uncanny effects to process and negotiate some specific forms of experiential shock and trauma related to the desire for, and the failure to secure, some important modes of shelter and home, and on both individual and collective levels; the work in question here takes the form of a collection of three lyric poems, all published since 2012, but meaningfully since the US housing crisis of 2008 and this long moment of national legislative failure concerning comprehensive immigration reform, and on the part of three Latinx poets of Mexican descent. The choice of the genre of especially *confessional* lyric poetry will also allow us to extend our analysis of Freud's argument concerning the relationship of representational realism to uncanny effects, given how differently the first-person lyrical address grounds us in a realist mode of aesthetic experience than what we conventionally expect from even the most autobiographically oriented first-person realist or naturalist fiction.

The three poems, in order of their appearance in their original book collections, are Eduardo Corral's "In Colorado My Father Scoured and Stacked Dishes" (in *Slow Lightning*, 2012), Rigoberto González's "Casa" (in *Unpeopled Eden*, 2013) and Ada Limón's "The Last Move" (in *Bright Dead Things*, 2015). Let me clarify as I begin to discuss these texts that in the same way that I'm cognizant that my long opening invocation and elaboration of Freud may be read as a fairly conservative critical act against whose surface conservatism I'd like to push back, I also don't mean to propose here any consideration of these three texts, or their writers or the cultural project(s) to which they might contribute, as an analogously conservative act of canon-formation, for all that it openly risks being read as such. Rather, I hope that the critical juxtaposition of Freud's admittedly canonical theoretical system with three such contemporary and variously (and I would add *consciously*) post- and anti-Freudian literary acts will serve to trouble any presumption that the very concept of the canonical, let alone any critical practice in its service, could possibly persist as either viable institutional scaffold for literary studies and literary criticism, or as either a motive or a goal for any cultural and intellectual work organizing itself around literary practice, going forward. And this, ironically, in the current moment we can all witness here today in the institutional, intellectual and ideological histories of US Latinx, and within it of US Latinx *literary*, studies, a moment in the latter that is, somewhat ironically, characterized by a kind of long-overdue return of critical interest in the ontology of the literary, in the lived practices of both the creative production of, and the creative engagement with, the "*Real*" of the text, and as typified by recent and still-emerging work from such intellectually diverse critic-scholars as Raúl Coronado, Paula Moya, and Ralph Rodriguez.[2]

To start with Corral's "In Colorado My Father Scoured and Stacked Dishes," we can observe in it a quality it shares with the other two poems under discussion here, which is how strikingly uncannily some of its fiercest effects play, and in simultaneously Freudian/Oedipal and anti-Freudian/anti-Oedipal ways. We can begin with the poles of gender-ambiguity that trouble any conventional oedipal reading: the speaker, whose own gender remains unnamed, addresses an audience of readers about a father whose first characterization is in a mode of traditionally feminine labor (he "scoured and stacked dishes"), and in a lyric that relentlessly refuses any reference to a mother. In a collection that so beautifully highlights queer male sexuality, the temptation to read "My Father"'s speaker as a male child is irresistible, but it's never explicitly authorized by the poem itself: even in the lines that come closest to narrating a dialogue between them ("Once, in a grove/ of saguaro, at dusk, I slept next to him. I woke/with his thumb in my mouth. ¿No qué no/tronabas pistolita?" and, later, the possible alternative imperative: "¡No mames!"), only the diminutive endearment "pistolita" might divulge the gender of the child speaker, but here the feminine gender of "pistola" in Spanish provides enough of a grammatical and semantic screen to keep things interesting, and to keep the general phallic economies of desire and anxiety in the text more openly at play. We know, of course, that in the division of labor into private versus public spaces in contemporary neoliberal North America, there's no guarantee that the work of "scouring and stacking dishes" lines up into any neatly gendered correspondences anyway: most of the dishwashers in our food service economy are likely male, and likely undocumented, and this might begin to explain in part why "My Father" seems so dead set against any focus on a recognizably stable domestic space, especially any such space defined by either matriarchal authority or maternal care. Spaces in "My Father," indoor or outdoor, tend to be spaces of public labor, migration or temporary refuge ("a Tex-Mex restaurant"; "a car trunk"; "a stable"; "a campfire"; "a grove of saguaro"; "the desert"); the only other references to interiors further fragment interiority ("Again and again," the speaker tells us, "I borrow his clothes"; "The heart can only be broken/once, like a window"; "When I walk through the desert, I wear his clothes") and most other references to exteriors map the complex geographical territoriality of mostly homeless and undocumented migration by naming the sites of labor that compel it (Colorado; Tex-Mex; Durango; Orizaba; the States; Tucson; Oregon). "My Father" the lyric therefore sings a song of illegal, unauthorized patrimony, a patrimony forbidden yet defined by the laws of nations, and the law of genre: "He's an illegal," the speaker tells us, then adds, "I'm an Illegal-American"; and later, the father "to entertain his cuates, around a campfire, … strummed a guitarra, sang corridos," arguably bestowing on the child-poet the same power of song, a power bestowed at once as burden and gift, like the borrowed clothes, the "shirt" whose "buttons" the "gaze of the moon/ stitches" to the speaker's "skin."

That lunar "gaze," along perhaps with the "car trunk" that serves as womb and coffin "smuggl[ing]" the father into illegal "life" and social death in "the States," may be as close to a maternal (let alone feminine) reference as we get in "My Father"; by contrast, Rigoberto González's "Casa" opens with the following violently negative invocation of the maternal: "I am not your mother, I will not be moved/by the grief or gratitude of men/who weep like orphans at my door." The title of González's lyric signals what the text of the poem evinces: "Casa" names the speaker of the piece, in this case a house whose sole mission across the arc of the poem's performative elaboration seems to be the explicit repudiation of reading any "house" as a "home." If Corral's poem maintains a consistent correspondence between unauthorized migration and a general condition of homelessness, González's flips the analogy: the constant threat of housing precarity becomes the touchstone for additional repudiations and refusals of the desire or attempt to secure shelter or claim a home, across all forms of local, regional, national, cultural and even spiritual belonging. And unlike "My Father"'s surprisingly rhetorically more conventional lyrical mode, "Casa" enacts a far more violent rhetorical gesture in opting as often as it does for a cruelly imperative voice in its address to its reader:

Come in and kneel or sit or stand,
the burden of your weight won't lessen
no matter the length of your admission.
Tell me anything you want, I have to listen
but don't expect me to respond

when you tell me you have lost your job
or that your wife has found another love
or that your children took their laughter
to another town.

"Casa"'s strategy of address thus situates the reader in the position of the victimized subject of forces (both dramatic and historical) beyond our control: we enter the poem the only way the poem allows, obediently and submissively, on our knees, a passive audience to a speaker who explicitly refuses to respond to us, regardless of our complaints, which here range from the loss of work, to the loss of love, to the loss of family, and eventually to a loss of home that later in the poem explodes into the mass eviction of a systemic housing crash: "Farewell, cold bed that breaks its bones/in protest to eviction or foreclosure or/whatever launched this grim parade/of exits." Significantly unlike "My Father," "Casa" bears the marks of its supposed Latinx provenance surprisingly lightly: beyond the use of the Spanish word for house in the title, the rest of the poem seems to want to paint a more general picture of that "grim parade/of exits," a picture that might just as aptly describe a process of mass migration out of a country as a process of mass eviction in a cratering housing market, but in both cases stopping short of specifying which country, or which market.

"Casa" thus works as an extended act of refusal of both lyrical and political sentiment; the title announces the confusion in Spanish between "casa" and "hogar," where "casa" in Spanish can sometimes connote "home" in a way that "house" in English doesn't (there is no equivalent in English for "mi casa es su (or tu) casa," not even "make yourself at home" works to translate that sentiment), and allows that confusion to stand without resolution. The discursive elaboration of figures in the rest of the poem also tends away, as we have already seen, from the sentimental language of family and home, to the much more instrumental terminology of policy and law. ("I granted/nothing," the speaker asserts later, "to the immigrant or exile/that I didn't give a bordercrosser or a native/born.") But that particular discursive migration, at once taxonomic and tonal, from the sentimental to the instrumental, already muddled in the ambiguity of the poem's title, encounters a corresponding muddling in another term, appearing just after the lines housing their collection of "immigrant" and "exile," "bordercrosser" and "native/born": there the speaker declares, "I am not a fairytale castle. Though I/used to be, in some distant land inhabited/by dreamers now extinct. Who knows what happened there?" One operant term here, of course, is "dreamers"; if "Casa" by this point has already marked itself as a dirge for the age of housing's collapse, its later stanzas expand that lament to include the collapse of all hope of meaningful comprehensive immigration reform in the latter days of the Obama era. That lament is largely sounded in the confusion of the sentimental with the instrumental in the terminology of the by-now decades-old DREAM Act, which discursively renders the "alien minors" it seeks to "develop, relieve and educate" more as "dreamers," that is, as sentimental aspirants to some residual notion of an American "dream," and less so as practical supplicants to the instrumental protections of proposed changes to existing yet recalcitrant law. The other operant term or perhaps phrase here, however, is "now extinct," which supplants the confusion in "dreamers" with the starker clarity, the absolute finality, of an extinction that feels, more than environmental, pointedly existential. The shock of "Casa" returns from its opening lines to its closing suggestion: that the worst, for all that it may still be to come, has also already happened, and for all that we may, in this "now," persist in remaining, it was a worst that we failed to survive. The poem, through its speaker, can only finally confess, "I am just a house,/a structure without soul for those whose/patron saints are longing and despair."

If "My Father" and "Casa" both work in different ways to render themselves "structure[s] without soul," to use their specific modes of lyrical being and lyrical work to evacuate themselves, via different "shock" effects, of any conventionally sentimental meaning regarding prevailing public discourses of home-ownership, aspirational migration or national belonging, Ada Limón's "The Last Move" (2015) attacks similar sentiments and the ideological myths they buttress not by standing outside the space of positive inclusion to witness its failure and collapse, but instead by situating its speaker, and its drama, fully within that space of supposedly successful inclusion. The "Last" in the title provides the poem with a defining tension, but only between the finality of a "last" move suggesting the speaker and her partner have arrived at a place of meaningful and lasting emotional fulfillment where they might permanently land, and the anxious impermanence of a "last" that only connotes a previous move in a sequence that offers no promise of ending, of landing anywhere (for) good. If Limón's title does some of the work of meaningful evacuation by preferring to name the common substantive for changing homes (a "move" here more specific than mere random motion, but also a "move" that stops short of promising "mobility," or prompting further "migration," or inspiring anything as ambitious as a "movement") over the home itself, the rest of the poem turns fully inward, to the concentric circles of interiority from the speaker's head to the speaker's house, in its troubled stagings of an anxious, if shared, inhabitation. The drama of "The Last Move" has mostly to do with a clearly cis-female speaker's negotiation of life choices recently made in the context of her love of and commitment to a cis-male partner (including a move from New York City to rural Kentucky), but the language of the poem pretty strenuously tests all the elements of cis-hetero-, or any other kind of, -normativity that situation might invoke. The speaker's apparently loving surrender to her partner, and to their partnership, occasions a series of expressions of splitting and doubling in her own subjectivity that could have been lifted verbatim from the general text of psychoanalysis:

> Hardwood planks under the feet, a cord to the sky.
> What is it to go to a *We* from an *I*?
>
> Each time he left for an errand, the walls
> would squeeze me in. I cried over the nonexistent bathmat, wet
>   floor of him,
> how south we were, far away in the outskirts ...
>
> This is Kentucky, not New York, and I am not important.
>
> This was before we got the dog even, and before I trusted
>
> the paralyzing tranquilizer of love stuck
> in the flesh of my neck.
>
> Back home, in my apartment, another woman lived there.

The "other woman" mentioned here is in part the speaker's former self, still at "home" in a past and a space now abandoned thanks to the "paralyzing tranquilizer of love stuck" in the speaker's "neck," a woman past rescue and revival beyond her occasional reappearance, first as memory, then later, in the poem's closing image, as the haunting, doubling uncanny, and un-homely residual of a violent repression at once belonging and not belonging to the speaker:

> Somewhere, I had heard that, after noting the lack
> of water pressure in an old hotel in Los Angeles,
> they found a woman's body at the bottom
> of the cistern.
>
> Imagine, just thinking the water was low, just wanting
> to take a shower.
>
> After that, when the water would act weird,
> spurt or gurgle, I'd imagine a body, a woman, a me
> just years ago, freely single, happily unaccounted for,
> at the lowest curve of the water tower.
>
> Yes, and over and over,
> I'd press her limbs down with a long pole
> until she was still.

The actual young woman whose body was discovered in that hotel water tank was Elisa Lam, a Chinese-Canadian tourist with a history of mental illness who had disappeared while staying at downtown LA's Cecil Hotel in early 2013 and who was not discovered where she had died for almost three weeks; the cause of her death was ruled accidental and likely the result of bipolar disorder.

Knowing the historical source of Limón's anecdote opens a door into a larger history of migration, gender and disability than we can explore here, but I'm hoping we can invite Elisa Lam into what little remains of our discussion in this section to underscore the stakes and the wages involved in committed poetry's responses to actual violence in our actual world, even when that violence occurs within the most intimate space of a troubled individual's acts of self-harm, but also when the violence is systemic, mindless of intimacy, individuality and domesticity, and only concerned with the larger, categorical mass effects of exclusion, displacement and even extermination. Across "My Father," "Casa," and "Move," we have witnessed varying scales of cruelty and indifference, yet also of care, even love, staged between imagined individual figures in their respective local dramas, and also always between and among poet and speaker and reader, but also across larger historical and political stages. I want to conclude here, however, with the concrete poetic image with which Limón leaves us, an image at once of reflexive self-harm (the speaker ensuring her former, freer self remains dead by drowning her again and again), the arguably "cruel" if evocative use on Limón's part of Lam's body, of the memory of her tragic and pathetic death, to occasion the characterization of that self-harm through the mediation of an evocatively abject "other," to the larger symbolic and dramatic resonances of a lyrical account of a normative domesticity whose enabling psychic act is a violent, repressive (female) self-sacrifice, and even, perhaps, to a larger theoretical force of illogic, one that exceeds the traditional, canonical psychoanalytic dependence, for any future elaboration of the uncanny as an aesthetic effect of any general or specific creative practice, on cis-hetero-patriarcho-normative forms of identification, projection, repression and cathexis, a force of illogic that still allows for the emergence of productively uncanny effects, but now through the radical evacuation of all conventional, authorized and authorizing logics of gender, generation, and sexuality; family, home, and nation; and genre, canon, and literature, altogether.

NOTES

1. Another conceptual thread that we might have pulled out of Freud's essay would have traced more explicitly at its vivid evocation of the corporal, erotic dynamics of the family romance as specifically elaborated there, but also as an exemplary symptom of its operation across the body of Freud's work. "It often happens," Freud observes, "that neurotic men declare that they feel there is something uncanny about the female genital organs. This *unheimlich* place, however, is the entrance to the former *Heim* [home] of all human beings, to the place where each one of us lived once upon a time and in the beginning. There is a joking saying that 'Love is home-sickness'; and whenever a man dreams of a place or a country and says to himself, while he is still dreaming: 'this place is familiar to me. I've been here before,' we may interpret the place as being the mother's genitals or her

body. In this case too, the *unheimlich* is what was once *heimisch*, familiar; the prefix 'un' ['*un-*'] is the token of repression." See Freud, *Standard Edition*, Vol. XVII, Trans. Lytton Strachey (Hogarth Press, 1955): 245. This language especially provides fairly explosive counterpoint to the sentence ("I am not your mother.") that opens poet Rigoberto González's remarkable lyric, "Casa," which we read closely in this section. It also absolutely haunts the feminist and queer of color deconstructions of hetero-patriarchal domesticity that we'll encounter in all three poems under discussion here. The three poetry collections we will draw from here are: Eduardo Corral, *Slow Lightning* (Yale UP, 2012); González, Rigoberto, *Unpeopled Eden* (Four Way Books, 2013); Ada Limón, *Bright Dead Things* (Milkweed Editions, 2015).

2. See Coronado, *The World Not to Come*; Moya, *The Social Imperative*; and Ralph Rodríguez, *Latinx Literature Unbound*.

CHAPTER 7

(Latinx) Literature's Work: Between Being and Becoming, Product and Practice

Abstract This final section concludes the larger discussion by returning to a combined focus on the articulation of the paired concepts of *latinidad* and *literature* to argue finally for a critical recalibration of Latinx literary criticism's inter-implicated and more than simultaneous commitments to both. It uses work by Horacio Legrás and Jean-Marie Schaeffer to trace the return of critical interest in the complex material, practical, laborious ontology of the literary, in the wake of but not necessarily in opposition to deconstruction, to model an alternative critical methodology for Latinx literary studies. The section closes by turning briefly to a story by Junot Díaz to demonstrate how this methodology might already be in performative practice in the literary work itself.

Keywords Literary education · Literary studies · Literary practice · Ontology · Work · Labor · Materiality

Literature, literary practice, of course, at least continues to work, and at most even thrive, both in and beyond the Latin American and US Latinx contexts, as does the practice that still concedes to call itself

This essay hopes to make its own implicit case for the momentousness, for US Latinx literary studies as a field, of the turn from the first to the second decade of the twenty first century. Without offering an exhaustive list of publications,

© The Author(s) 2019
R. L. Ortiz, *Latinx Literature Now*, Literatures of the Americas,
https://doi.org/10.1007/978-3-030-04708-5_7

literary studies. Perhaps in the US Latinx context which mostly concerns the present discussion, and which took so much of our attention in the preceding sections, that practice remains even in the current moment caught in its own impasseable state of critical undecidability, either too early or too late to make coherent sense in its current formation.[1] Perhaps, too, it remains beholden, for better or worse, to the pull of a cultural politics of social restitution and social justice that favors the call of *latinidad* as politicized identity over the disciplinary (and philosophical) demands of *literature* as discursive material practice still-awaiting just accounts of both its ontological unfolding and its viable epistemological capture. Perhaps too, however, some models of how such an ethically, socially responsible critical encounter with the literary in its actual, material being might actually exist, and even in the space of what we can (perhaps) call Latin(x) American literary studies in a post-testimonial, post-historical mode.

we can at least suggest that, beginning in 2007 with the appearance of Raphael Dalleo and Elena Machado Sáez's *The Latino/a Canon and the Emergence of Post-sixties Literature* (Palgrave Macmillan, 2007), and following up with Ilán Stavans' *Norton Anthology of Latino Literature* in 2011, then Kirsten Silva Gruesz's *PMLA* review of the Stavans project in 2012, then Suzanne Bost and Frances Aparicio's *Routledge Companion to Latino/a Literature* (Routledge, 2013), to John Morán González's *Cambridge Companion to Latina/o-American Literature* (Cambridge UP, 2016), the field of US Latinx literary studies has certainly experienced an intense and perhaps definitive institutionalization, certainly at least as an academic publishing phenomenon, but also in perhaps less measurable ways as these projects facilitate the teaching of US Latinx Literature courses, organize if not settle what might serve as forms of foundational knowledge for scholarly and critical (and even creative?) work yet to come, and even more indirectly encourage the hiring of more faculty to teach in the field, as more university departments discover the depth, value, and legitimacy of that field, and start finally to feel the urgent need to teach it to an increasingly diverse, and increasingly *Latinx*, university student body. It is not the task of the present discussion, however, to replicate the work of these volumes, each of which opens with a helpful, informative introduction that makes the case for that project's respective function and value, usually doing so by situating its specific contribution to the field in the context of the varying contributions of the other volumes listed here.

Horacio Legrás' *Literature and Subjection: The Economy of Writing and Marginality in Latin America* (2008), for example, from its opening pages trains its vigilant, critical attention on what it calls "the dynamic by which literature must look to its own arsenal for weapons that may allow it to negate its historical domestication" for hegemonic purposes in undertaking its "cultural study of the literary form," because, as Legrás warns, any "historical account of literature unable to pose [such] theoretical problems ... will remain imperialist and colonialist while pretending to be representative and emancipatory" (1–2).[2] For Legrás, any responsible and viably productive critical encounter with what he calls "the being of the literary" (5) must travel through the ontological before making its way through the epistemological on its way eventually toward any critical turns that might then pivot toward whatever contributions it might make to the effect of transformative change, toward any hoped-for further approach, that is, *toward* justice. He inaugurates that process in his own project by enumerating what he calls "the two constitutive and essential components of the literary experience: its transcendental aim and its actual form," and then elaborating from this grounding axiomatic the following caveats: "Any 'transcendental' interrogation of literature remains naïve if it fails to address how the primary disposition of the literary leads it to articulate the goal of culture as an apparatus of capture and adaptation. [While a]t the same time," he avers, "no cultural inquiry into the politics of literature remains valid if it fails to account for the singularity and autonomy of literature" (3). It is in part the suggestion of the present discussion that this in some ways paradoxical/dialectical tension of the literary as at once "transcendental aim" and "actual form" takes a specific shape in contemporary projects of minority-identitarian literary expression, and perhaps not exclusively in the post-multicultural, post-Obama US context, given how simultaneously the questions of "aim" and "form" seem to arise.

What Legrás worries about in his work regarding "the intimacies of state power and the literary imagination" (3) might in the contemporary post-multicultural US context look more like the concerns regarding a hegemonic practice of multicultural diversity and identity studies primarily decentered because farmed out to the university as itself "an apparatus of capture and adaptation." For Legrás, therefore, this "being" of literature is always doubled, a "dual being ... [as] an institution and ... an instituting power" (4), where something like an instituting and inaugural literary practice always precedes any institutionalization of, say, a canon, or a formal, official knowledge about that canon, and about whatever tradition or history such a canon helps to anchor or ground. What's most valuable in Legrás' work for the purposes of the present discussion, therefore, is his meticulous tracing through all of its phases of the dialectical and irresolvable operations of this double being, "literature" as both (ontologically) instituting practice and (epistemologically) instituted knowledge about that practice.

Legrás, understandably, is careful to account for the specific modes in which these operations of dual being played themselves out in the Latin American context: "The representational mode that fell to Latin American literature for most of the modern period," he tells us, "depends on the simple fact that the representing and the represented instances belong to different orders. For this reason, since the instantiation of national literatures, the translation of the local and the status of the universal have constituted a persistent problem" (6). That problem, however, and in its very persistence, becomes for Legrás the ground for further critical elaboration: "Literature," he observes, "has long been Latin America's explicative ontology . . , [one] that constitutes the world according to a set of rules that precedes its involvement with the facticity of events or the brute materiality of life," and thereby entailing that "whenever Latin American literature has tried to portray that identity between thinking and being, it has been denounced as an agent of violence and domination" (7). Legrás sustains the logic of this critique of mid-twentieth-century modernist, nationalist literary-critical practice all the way through the introductory chapter of his book, and in its concluding passages he offers both an updating of it that might apply beyond postmodern, transnational and contemporary Latin American contexts, and an alternative account of the material ontology of literary practice that continues to exceed the ambitions of state- and otherwise official-, institutional hegemonic attempts to regulate it and (to claim) to know it.

The first of these observations has direct relevance to the work of US Latinx and other ethnic studies projects to the extent that it cautions against the logics of official and institutional inclusion via more democratically representative forms of recognition that often drive the discourses of diversity and identity knowledge across contemporary multicultural societies and other transnational institutional and social formations driven by neoliberal globalization. "[R]ecognition," Legrás tells us, "is above all a strategy through which power re-asserts itself in the minute details of everyday life. The recognition," therefore, "granted by the state (or by literature as a state apparatus) is never a gift, but a loan that is finally collected in kind. In this economy of reflexion and return," Legrás concludes, "the state provides recognition in exchange for rec- ognition ... Every recognition granted by the state empowers the state's own imaginary constitution"; a "structure" of so decidedly uneven a Hegelian intersubjective exchange, he insists, "is destined to progress via waves of violence and suppression in those regions, like Latin America, where the heterogeneity of the society cannot be easily reconciled with the centripetal impulses of nation-state formation" (22). So while the US Latinx literary-critical establishment might want to keep one eye always on some guarded, vigilant demand for a representative, conceptual, cat- egorical institutionalization, especially in higher education academic set- tings, and via official forms of recognition, we might also want to keep an eye toward those spaces, constituted contingently by and as risk and accident, where something like what Danticat calls the work of the itiner- ant, precarious, "immigrant" artist might be able to happen, and in ways that necessarily elude, exceed or at least trouble too-interested forms of institutional and official capture.

Legrás' second observation attempts to describe both the space where, and the process by which, literature's work can happen such that the dialectic between freedom and power in which that work is always caught tilts more toward the former than the latter. "There is common ground," he explains, "to art and labor that we express through the notion of work. Like labor, art and literature are primary ways of inhab- iting the world. This is why we keep going back to them, expecting to find in them the disclosure of a productive dimension that, bringing us full circle in the system of our determinations, will provide a genuine possibility for overcoming the postcolonial heritage that keeps logic and ontology separate in our experience of the world" (22–23). Legrás' pro- ject thus allows us to take the full measure of the distance traveled in two short decades, from the moment of Beverley's polemic in *Against Literature* to the still-emerging critical-philosophical moment in which we find ourselves now, which Legrás's work hails as far back as 2008, and which involves fields of practice beyond even the capacious "borders" of Latin American literary studies, a moment which may yet effect a return, productive and not redemptive, *to* literature, that "primary way of inhab- iting the world" whose potential for transformation of that world we may have not yet actually managed to exhaust.[3]

Legrás' suggestions from 2008 have taken more ambitiously comprehensive form in more recent work in a reconstituted field of a posttheoretical (and admittedly European) philosophy of literature, here represented by Terry Eagleton's *The Event of Literature* (2012) and Jean-Marie Schaeffer's "Literary Studies and Literary Experience" (2013). Two phases of Eagleton's discussion in the book will engage us here, one that echoes Austin and Derrida in accounting for literary practice through the concepts of performative act and performative force, and a second that offers a complementary account to Legrás' (and Danticat's) of artistic, creative practice as active work, as a "primary way of being [and doing] in the world"; with Schaeffer, we will encounter one productive response to ongoing critical anxieties about the ideological motivations behind, and consequences of, inadequately self-critical forms of institutional[-izing] literary-studies practice, and then turn to his account of readerly practice as itself offering a complementary mode of "primary" being in the world with its own claims to potentially transformative (productive, forceful) effects on that world. "Literary speech acts," Eagleton explains in the chapter of his book on "The Nature of Fiction," "belong to the larger class of verbal acts known as performatives, which do not describe the world but accomplish something in the act of saying ... A work of fiction ... consists of a set of realities which have no existence apart from its act of enunciation ... [;] Fiction accomplishes its ends in the act of saying. What is true in the novel is true simply by virtue of the discursive act itself. Yet it can have a palpable effect on reality" (131–132).[4] One can return here to Derrida's larger argument in "Signature, Event, Context" that what most fully obtains in the performative act of utterance has less to do with any intended communication of a constative meaning from the writer to the reader, but instead some more effective, active force imbedded in the act as act; one could also return to Danticat's demand, in her appropriative echo of Camus, of an art that convinces, stipulating here that conviction and persuasion primarily operate in the world rhetorically, as act and strategy, rather than in some communicative network of information, via modes of constative, semantic transmission.[5]

Eagleton devotes considerable attention in his chapter on fiction to this application of speech-act theory to his larger analysis of literary practice, and while he does not land definitively or exclusively in that camp, he clearly appreciates the value of its contribution to the larger philosophical project that engages his book, and that engages us here.[6] And from this grounding in a kind of performative ontology of the literary utterance as act, Eagleton can complement aspects of the account of the ontology of literary practice that we saw from Legrás. As "performative acts," Eagleton argues, the literary utterances that texts are "can also be powerful interventions in the world, accomplishing momentous changes and producing tangible effects," and thereby standing, in their most positive and self-constituting articulations, as radical performances of "human freedom," which for Eagleton "is not a question of being bereft of determinants, but of making them one's own, turning them into the grounds of one's self-constitution" (138–140).[7] For Eagleton, then, bodies and actions make worlds upon worlds, and any productive action on the part of anybody can only be so constituted as utterance with consequent force, consequent effect; "Bodies and language," he insists, "are ways of being in the midst of things, rather than obstacles that shut us out from them. It is by being 'inside' of a body or language," he concludes, "that we can encounter one another and intervene in what is misleadingly known as the outside world" (143). Eagleton then expands on this model of literary practice as embodied action in the chapter entitled "Strategies," where he more explicitly politicizes the model by engaging with the work of, among others, Kenneth Burke and Fredric Jameson in elaborating the analysis of the literary act as critical, creative, strategic, interventional utterance that seizes the materials of discourse to speak differently than how prevailing ideologies already speak and determine and enforce their limits on the sayable.

For both Burke and Jameson, these critical performative operations take place much more powerfully at the level of form than the level of content, which provides Eagleton with the necessary point of connection with speech-act theory, and which allows him the formulation of a "complex view of the relations between text and ideology, or text and history," that the present essay has already been developing through its discussions of Danticat, Alvarez, Beverley, and Trouillot, among others. "[T]ext and ideology, ... text and history" do not, Eagleton argues, "stand ... to each other in a relationship of reflection, reproduction, correspondence, homology and the like, but as alternative facets of a single symbolic practice. The work itself," he goes on, "is to be seen not as a reflection of a history external to it, but as a strategic labor,—as a way to setting to work *on* a reality which, in order to be accessible to it, must somehow be contained within it" (170). This model of the work of literature as consequential action in turn provides Eagleton with the basis upon which to build his more ambitious analysis of the general coincidence of the realms of labor and the symbolic:

Human labor is itself a mode of sense-making, a way of organizing reality coherently enough to satisfy our needs; but for it to be truly effective, we also need a mode of meta-sense-making, some more speculative
form of reflection on the world our labor and language have opened up.
This, all the way from myth and philosophy to art, religion, and ideology, is the realm of the symbolic ... If art is one of the ways we subdue
the world to sense and if such sense-making is necessary for our survival, then the non-pragmatic is ultimately the name of the pragmatic.
Yet it may also be that the opposite is true—that historically speaking,
the pragmatic (or realm of necessity) must be overtaken by the non-
pragmatic (the domain of freedom). This, in a word, is the hope of
Marxism ... The wealth which at present we toil to produce might be
used to free us from toil. (179)

Eagleton's language here returns us to Edwidge Danticat's characterization of what "immigrant" artists do as work. And it can also begin to
pose the possibility that what readers do, all attentive, serious readers in
one respect, but certainly professionally trained readers, critics, and scholars, in some more specialized respect, is active, productive consequential work, evental/eventive activity that interacts with creative work not
exclusively in some relationship of irreducible alterity, where criticism and
scholarship only appear "outside" and "after" the literary objects and acts
to which they can only respond, but in ways that activate in modes of
productive simultaneity new processes of creation and transformation in
collaboration with the artistic work.

Eagleton's language here also resonates rather dramatically with an
important passage from the work of the Dominican–American fiction
writer, Junot Díaz. The concluding lines of "The Cheater's Guide to
Love," itself the final story of his 2012 collection, *This Is How You Lose
Her*, read as follows:

The next day you look at the new pages. For once you don't want to burn
them or give up writing forever.

It's a start, you say to the room.

That's about it. In the months that follow you bend to the work, because
it feels like hope, like grace—and because you know in your lying cheater's
heart that sometimes a start is all we ever get. (213)[8]

As the present discussion (finally!) closes, its writer hopes his patient reader appreciates how much of the preceding work has been itself a series of readings, often close, hopefully careful, and, in their direct and detailed attention to the texts read, perhaps overly, compulsively citational. As Junot Díaz models for us in the passage from "The Cheater's Guide," we know that the "you" bending toward her or his "work" exceeds the self-referencing (and male) writer/narrator/protagonist anchoring the movements internal to the story and its fictions, if only to the extent that such a writer, in also being the primary addressee of the second-person "you" of the narrative's governing rhetorical performance, prefigures all possible future addressees to come, all of them readers, some of them critics and scholars, hence serving as the threshold mechanism for the unending process of interlocution that will be the text's active afterlife, what will (always) continue to constitute the text as event. We all, therefore, should find ourselves happily "bend[ing] to the work ... because it feels like hope, like grace."

As readers, we thus participate in the part of the experiential event of the literary that takes up Jean-Marie Schaeffer's attention in his 2013 essay, "Literary Studies and Literary Experience"; "Reading," Schaeffer argues there, "introduces us to the real and it even trains us to confront it, but without sanctioning our actions directly (or even dramatically).[9] The imaginative immersion that is part and parcel of literary fiction is thus a specific and irreplaceable mode of understanding and experimentation. No analysis," he goes on, "can give us this imaginative understanding. It is accessible only through the direct experience of immersion in its universe." This immersion in a deeply imagined "reality," Schaeffer tells us, comprises the "aesthetic relationship" for the reader, "a form of human conduct in which the playing out of attention (perceptive, linguistic, etc.) is the central concern," and where, "because attention itself, and reading as an act, is the goal of our activity, the operative principle is no longer the minimalization, but rather the maximalization, of our attentional investments" (279). As we all, therefore, bend to all the work still to come, we might want to begin by checking our own habits toward a too-specific training of our attention toward the limiting (and mostly political) hermeneutic that we expect our colleagues and our field to expect from us, and to pursue, perhaps more fully than we have before, that "maximalization" of our "attentive investments" that our most fully, really immersive encounters with richly imagined (Latinx) literary realities provoke in us.

The life, the being, the experience we may most importantly rescue with such a capacious reopening of our critical attention to the fullest manifestation of the event we want to call "US Latinx literature" might be our own, but it will also model an important, even vital, opening to being for all the readers we in turn encounter (and train) along the way. "In the life of each person," Schaeffer observes, "the importance of reading literary works, whether they are narrative, lyric (poetic) or dramatic, is not found in inferences drawn reflexively from the work, but in the movement of our mental universe operated by the experience of reading itself … this efficacy is not due to some epistemic, even ontological, election of literature. It is rather an effect of the immersive procedures of the story, of the polyphony and polysemy of the poetic enunciations, as well as the actantial simulation of the theater … Reading," Schaeffer thus insists, "does not need to be connected a posteriori to life: *it is a moment of life, a lived experience as real as any other*" (281). It is this last point (emphasis mine) that perhaps the defining critical (and ideological) impulses of US Latinx literary-critical practice have for too long ignored, dismissed, or agonized over to an excessive and detrimental degree. Literature has perhaps too often served for us as an alibi, a convenient access point to the study of US *latinidad*, but at best only convenient, even, really, contingent; what we have to imagine going forward, what we might imagine desiring, perhaps even working to make happen, is that possible world where no one "attentional investment" in our reading of US Latinx literature trumps any other, if it is for whatever responsible reason worthy of that attention. Our commitment to *literature* should at least equal, or perhaps commensurate and complement, our commitment to *latinidad*, if we are to profess ourselves as practitioners of the field, and that dialectic of commitments should, if we bend honestly, responsibly, and happily to the work it invites us to do, feel "like hope, like grace."

NOTES

1. See Kirsten Silva Gruesz's important 2012 review of Ilán Stavans' *Norton Anthology of Latino Literature* ("What Was Latino Literature?," in *PMLA* 127: 2 [March 2012], 335–341). The question of the ongoing "Latin Americanization" of the US Latinx literary field offers Silva Gruesz grounds for both what travels through her take-no-prisoners critique of Stavans and what survives in her own analysis as the potential for redemption in certain aspects of US Latinx literary-critical and -scholarly practice

in the current moment. She explicitly faults Stavans for assembling a team of coeditors the majority of whom hold their highest degrees in Spanish or Latin American studies, and for concentrating in the early sections of the *Norton Anthology* on the strictly Latin American colonial and postcolonial roots of Latinx literature in mostly Hispanophone discourses predating an Anglophone US Latinx modernity that really does not appear in that volume until the twentieth century. This failure or refusal on the *Norton* team's part more fully to anchor US Latinx literary history in its US American context means, for Silva Gruesz, that they "present an authoritative canon for a body of literature that doesn't yet have a literary history" (336) by borrowing a "history" from outside its claimed national space, and often without direct reference to that particular national history. "What none of the [*Norton*'s organizing] periods do," she argues, "is to mark out a social project, akin to ending slavery or segregation, around which the category of Latino literature might organize itself," which leads eventually to her rather bracing conclusion, that: "the *Norton* ... has arrived on the scene either twenty years too early—before its compilers had coherent narratives about the tradition to offer—or twenty years too late, past the moment when ethnic literature could represent a collective social project rather than a market-driven instrument for managing minoritized populations" (340).

2. In a footnote attached to an earlier section I situated Legrás's 2008 project in the genealogy of Latin American literary and cultural studies work to which it primarily responds, and while readers familiar with that work will appreciate the specificity of its critique of literature's national-hegemonic work in twentieth century Latin American contexts, I want at least to suggest here that earlier iterations of US Latinx literary studies have shared those mostly politically- and ideologically-based concerns about the potentially exclusionary and elitist uses of what pass for "naïve" forms of literary study. For this reason I attempt as I do here to fold Legras' work into a critique of US Latinx literary studies that runs through much of the material listed in that footnote above. A useful if more general critique of this process in its US-based contexts can be found in David Palumbo-Liu, Ed.'s collection *The Ethnic Canon: Histories, Institutions and Interventions* (University of Minnesota Press, 1995); a much more recent but similarly general and useful critique runs through Robin Wiegman's *Object Lessons* (Duke UP, 2012), also mentioned in an earlier footnote.

3. While this discussion relies mostly on the work of Legrás, Eagleton, and Schaeffer to manage its core critical interventions, it does claim an intentional if here mostly indirect and implicit engagement with important recent contributions to the larger scholarly conversation about the function, purpose, and value of literary criticism, including Joseph North's

Literary Criticism: A Concise Political History (Harvard UP, 2017); Elisabeth Anker and Rita Felski's collection *Critique and Post-critique* (Duke UP, 2017); Felski's *The Limits of Critique* (University of Chicago Press, 2015); and *The Uses of Literature* (Blackwell, 2008), the special issue of *Representations* edited by Stephen Best and Sharon Marcus entitled *The Way We Read Now* (*Representations* 108) (Fall 2009), etc.

4. This chapter of Eagleton's book also contains one of the more clarifying arguments available on the philosophical status of fiction, and of literature more generally: "Fiction," Eagleton tell us, "is an ontological category, not in the first place a literary genre. A passionately sincere lyric is as fictional as *Lolita*. Fiction is a question of how texts behave, and of how we treat them, not primarily of genre, and certainly not ... of whether they are true or false" (111). Readers will encounter an even more nuanced and elaborated analysis of the ontological and phenomenological dimensions of both the production of and encounter with fiction in the Schaeffer essay under discussion here. "[T]he nature of fiction," Schaeffer argues, "depends on a pragmatics of representations and not on literary syntax ... it is not an intrinsically literary reality, but the implementation of a mental ability that is part of the common stock of human behaviors," which together comprise a battery of forms of "fictional competence" that include "playful pretense, mimetic immersion, and analog modeling"; "Fictional modeling," he goes on, "conforms *in general* to plausible lines of force responding to conditions of representability that all experience must do so that we are able to live it as 'real experience.' In other words, fiction is not an *image* of the real world. It is a virtual exemplification of a possible being-in-the-world" (278).

5. This proposition directly responds to Kirsten Silva Gruesz's concerns (in her piece on Latin@ print culture in *The Routledge Companion*) about Latinx literary studies' flat-footed over-emphasis on the burdens of politically responsible (or politically correct) forms of representations of Latinx "experience." To quote Silva Gruesz directly: "Latino literary scholarship has historically emphasized social questions such as identity and the experience of marginality, yet the contextual evidence it gravitates towards is often limited to the author's life experiences and a general set of historical parameters that have shaped them. These contexts," she goes on, "tend to be subsumed into questions of *representation*: whether a particular novel does or doesn't offer a realistic or critical or visionary portrayal of Latino life." She concludes with the following important admonition to our entire guild: "Focusing on such textual representations can offer insight into the ways ideology works, but at the cost of overlooking the larger landscape surrounding the work's existence—including the vital question of who its audience really is, and why they should be drawn to this form of

cultural expression over others," thus in turn overlooking the rich history in which we all continue to participate: "the everyday workings of reading as social practice" (485). The current discussion also owes a debt to Silva-Gruesz's "The Once and Future Latino: Notes Toward a Literary History *todavía para llegar,*" in *Contemporary U.S. Latino Literary Criticism,* eds. Lyn Di Iorio Sandín and Richard Perez (Palgrave Macmillan, 2007: 115–142.)

6. Space limitations prohibit a more comprehensive account of Eagleton's analysis of the performativity of fiction in the present essay, but the following passage is worth condensing: "Fiction," Eagleton argues, "like performatives as a whole, is an event inseparable from its act of utterance. It has no support from outside itself, in the sense that what it asserts cannot be checked off in any important way against some independent testimony. In this sense, it is more like swearing than reporting a robbery. Fiction manufactures the very objects to which it appears to refer ... It looks like a report, but it is actually a piece of rhetoric ... a performative masquerading as a constative" (137).

7. Without having to take on the following historicist task itself, the current discussion will merely hypothesize here about the discernible historical effects of one provisional emergent formation, one among countless possible others, comprised of the following five moments: the production, transcription, and circulation of Rigoberta Menchú's 1984 *testimonio,* and the ideological, intellectual, and institutional debates that followed concerning its inclusion in US-based higher education curricula; the discovery in the early 1990s by Rosaura Sánchez and Beatrice Pita of the work of María Amparo Ruiz de Burton, and the resulting transformative reconfiguration of what comprised the historical "object" of US Latinx literary studies; the awarding of the 2007 Pulitzer Prize in fiction to Junot Díaz for *The Brief, Wondrous Life of Oscar Wao,* and the impact such a moment had on an already robust US Latinx literary-critical establishment with a decidedly anxious relationship to the kind of official canonization such a conferral of status might entail; the selection of Richard Blanco as Barack Obama's second inaugural poet, and the reading of "One Today" at the ceremony in January 2013, at that moment perhaps the most public evidence yet on national and global stages of US Latinx literature's participation in some larger processes of literary and cultural practice, and all the inevitable ideological concerns such a moment of course provokes, except: then came the explosive success of Lin-Manuel Miranda's Broadway musical *Hamilton* from its debut in 2015 on. *Hamilton* absolutely qualifies as US Latinx literature, even as it functions as so much else aesthetically, culturally, and historically, and therefore most powerfully poses as the horizon beyond which the present discussion, even some three years after the play's emergence, and during the ongoing critical backlash "against" it, can only hope to peer.

8. Díaz's place in this history took a serious, complex turn thanks to the publication (in *The New Yorker* on 16 April 2018) of an explosively confessional piece detailing his own experience as a victim of sexual assault as a child in the Dominican Republic, and the complex fallout of that violence over the rest of his life and literary career; immediately following that publication, a large group of writers and scholars have taken to social media and other venues in response to that piece, many of them women detailing Díaz's own troubling history of sexual misconduct toward them, others attempting to put the matter in critical contexts that might rescue Díaz from complete ostracism from public life while attending directly to the serious charges leveled against him. As of this writing, the controversy is open, ongoing, and nowhere near settlement.

9. In that essay, Schaeffer also provides a larger rationale that can apply to a field like Latinx literary studies as a larger structural and institutional project: "To the degree that a culture transforms itself by regarding itself as an object, through a process sometimes termed 'autopoetic,'" Schaeffer argues there, "this self-referentiality is the basis of the dynamic of culture as such. 'Literature' and the various counter-canons that have followed its dissolution is (was) a reality of this kind, and to choose a normative approach to literary phenomena is to inscribe oneself within this self-referential dynamic." Schaeffer goes on in that piece to offer an alternative approach to literary studies practice not to supplant the one just articulated, and so clearly descriptive of traditional *Latinx* literary studies practice, but to supplement, and complement, it. "[A]lthough the social mission of teaching literary phenomena as a worthwhile cultural ideal is an important one," he clarifies, "this mission must not be confused with the descriptive study of literary realities of which 'Literature' and various opposing counter-canons are but one aspect ... When a given reality includes regulative norms—which is true of literary practices—it stands to reason that a description of this reality includes a description and analysis of its mechanisms of evaluation and hierarchization. But when we study cultural reality in this way, the point is not to approve or reject the specific values it exhibits, but to describe it from an axiologically neutral perspective" (272–273).

BIBLIOGRAPHY

Acosta, Abraham. *Thresholds of Illiteracy: Theory, Latin American and the Crisis of Resistance*. New York, NY: Fordham UP, 2014.

Alvarez, Julia. *In the Time of the Butterflies*. New York: Plume, 1995.

Alvarez, Julia. "The Gladys Poems." *The Other Side/El Otro Lado*. New York: Plume, 1995. 5–21.

Alvarez, Julia. "Chasing the Butterflies." *Something to Declare*. New York: Plume, 1999. 197–209.

Alvarez, Julia. *In the Name of Salomé*. Chapel Hill, NC: Algonquin Books of Chapel Hill, 2000.

Anderson, Benedict. *Imagined Communities: Reflections on the Origin and Spread of Nationalism*. London: Verso, 1991.

Arenas, Reinaldo. *Before Night Falls: A Memoir*. Trans. Dolores Koch. New York, NY: Penguin Books, 1994.

Arias, Arturo, Ed. *The Rigoberta Menchú Controversy*. Minneapolis, MN: University of Minnesota Press, 2001.

Austin, J.L. *How to Do Things with Words*. Cambridge, MA: Harvard UP, 1962.

Avelar, Idelber. *The Untimely Present: Postdictatorial Latin American Fiction and the Task of Mourning*. Durham: Duke UP, 1999.

Beltrán, Cristina. *The Trouble with Unity: Latino Politics and the Creation of Identity*. Oxford: Oxford UP, 2010.

Beverley, John. *Against Literature*. Minneapolis, MN: University of Minnesota Press, 1993.

Beverley, John. *Testimonio: On the Politics of Truth*. Minneapolis, MN: University of Minnesota Press, 2004.

Beverley, John. *Latinamericanism After 9/11*. Durham, NC: Duke UP, 2011.

© The Editor(s) (if applicable) and The Author(s),
under exclusive licence to Springer Nature Switzerland AG 2019
R. L. Ortiz, *Latinx Literature Now*, Literatures of the Americas,
https://doi.org/10.1007/978-3-030-04708-5

Bost, Suzanne and Frances Aparicio, Eds. *The Routledge Companion to Latino/a Literature*. London: Routledge, 2013.

Butler, Judith. *The Psychic Life of Power: Theories in Subjection*. Stanford, CA: Stanford UP, 1997.

Butler, Judith. *Precarious Life: The Powers of Mourning and Violence*. London: Verso, 2004.

Butler, Judith. *Frames of War: When Is Life Grievable?* London: Verso, 2009.

Caminero-Santangelo, Marta. *On Latinidad: US Latino Literature and the Construction of Ethnicity*. Gainesville, FL: University of Florida Press, 2009.

Coronado, Raúl. *A World Not to Come: A History of Latino Writing and Print Culture*. Cambridge, MA: Harvard UP, 2013.

Corral, Eduardo. *Slow Lightning*. New Haven, CT: Yale UP, 2012.

Dalleo, Raphael and Elena Machado Sáez, Eds. *The Latino/a Canon and the Emergence of Post-sixties Literature*. New York, NY: Palgrave-Macmillan, 2007.

Danticat, Edwidge. *Brother, I'm Dying*. New York, NY: Alfred A. Knopf, 2007.

Danticat, Edwidge. *Create Dangerously: The Immigrant Artist at Work*. Princeton, NJ: Princeton UP, 2010.

Derrida, Jacques. *Limited Inc*. Trans. Samuel Weber. Chicago, IL: Northwestern UP, 1988.

Díaz, Junot. *This Is How You Lose Her*. New York, NY: Riverhead Books, 2012.

Eagleton, Terry. *The Event of Literature*. New Haven, CT: Yale UP, 2010.

Freud, Sigmund. *Standard Edition*, Vol. XVII. Trans. Lytton Strachey. London: Hogarth Press, 1955.

García, Cristina. *The Lady Matador's Hotel*. New York, NY: Simon & Schuster, 2010.

González, John Morán, Ed. *The Cambridge Companion to Latina/o-American Literature*. Cambridge: Cambridge UP, 2016.

González, John Morán and Laura Lomas, Eds. *The Cambridge History of Latina/o-American Literature*. Cambridge: Cambridge UP, 2016.

González, Rigoberto. *Unpeopled Eden*. New York: Four Way Books, 2013.

Gruesz, Kirsten Silva. *Ambassadors of Culture: The Transamerican Origins of Latino Writing*. Princeton, NJ: Princeton UP, 2002.

Gruesz, Kirsten Silva. "The Once and Future Latino: Notes Toward a Literary History *todavía para llegar*." In *Contemporary U.S. Latino Literary Criticism*, Eds. Lyn Di Iorio Sandín and Richard Perez. New York, NY: Palgrave Macmillan, 2007: 115–142.

Gruesz, Kirsten Silva. "What Was Latino Literature?" *PMLA* 127: 2 (March 2012), 335–341.

Guidotti-Hernández, Nicole M. *Unspeakable Violence: Remapping U.S. and Mexican National Imaginaries*. Durham, NC: Duke UP, 2011.

Haney-López, Ian F. *White by Law: The Legal Construction of Race*. New York, NY: New York UP, 1996.

Lazo, Rodrigo. *Writing to Cuba: Filibustering and Cuban Exiles in the United States*. Chapel Hill, NC: University of North Carolina Press, 2005.

Lazo, Rodrigo and Jesse Alemán, Eds. *The Latino Nineteenth Century*. New York, NY: New York UP, 2016.

Legrás, Horacio. *Literature and Subjection: The Economy of Writing and Marginality in Latin America*. Pittsburgh, PA: University of Pittsburgh Press, 2008.

Lima, Lázaro. *The Latino Body: Crisis Identities in American Literary and Cultural Memory*. New York, NY: New York UP, 2007.

Limón, Ada. *Bright Dead Things*. Minneapolis, MN: Milkweed Editions, 2015.

López-Calvo, Ignacio. *God and Trujillo: Literacy and Cultural Representations of the Dominican Dictator*. Gainesville: University Press of Florida, 2005.

Menchú, Rigoberta. *I, Rigoberta Menchú: An Indian Woman in Guatemala*. Ed. Elisabeth Burgos and Trans. Ann Wright. London, 1983.

Milián, Claudia. *Latining America: Black-Brown Passages and the Coloring of Latina/o Studies*. Athens, GA: Georgia UP, 2013.

Milián, Claudia, Ed. et al. *Theorizing LatinX*. Special issue of *Cultural Dynamics* 29: 3 (August 2017).

Moreiras, Alberto. *The Exhaustion of Difference: The Politics of Latin American Cultural Studies*. Durham, NC: Duke UP, 2001.

Moya, Paula. *The Social Imperative: Race, Close Reading, and Contemporary Literary Criticism*. Stanford, CA: Stanford UP, 2015.

Muñoz, José Esteban. *Cruising Utopia: The There and Then of Queer Futurity*. New York, NY: New York UP, 2009.

Oboler, Suzanne. *Ethnic Labels, Latino Lives: Identity and the Politics of (Re) Presentation in the United States*. Minneapolis, MN: University of Minnesota Press, 1995.

Ortiz, Ricardo L. "Edwidge Danticat's *Latinidad*: The Farming of Bones and the Cultivation of (Fields of) Knowledge." In *Aftermaths: Exile, Migration, and Diaspora Reconsidered*, eds. Marcus Bullock and Peter Paik, Rutgers UP, 2008.

Ortiz, Ricardo L. "On (Our-) American Ground: Caribbean-Latino-Diasporic Cultural Production and the Post-National 'Guantanamera'," in *Social Text* 94 (Spring 2008), 3–28.

Ortiz, Ricardo L. "Writing the Haitian Diaspora: The Trans-National Contexts of Edwidge Danticat's *The Dew Breaker*." In *Imagined Transnationalism: US Latino/a Literature, Culture and Identity*, eds. Kevin Concannon, Francisco A. Lomelí and Marc Priewe. New York: Palgrave, 2010: 237–256.

Palumbo-Liu, David, Ed. *The Ethnic Canon: Histories, Institutions and Interventions*. Minneapolis, MN: University of Minnesota Press, 1995.

Rodriguez, Juana María. *Queer Latinidad: Identity Practices, Discursive Spaces*. New York, NY: New York UP, 2003.

Rodriguez, Ralph E. *Latinx Literature Unbound: Undoing Ethnic Expectation.* New York, NY: Fordham UP, 2018.

Rodríguez, Richard. *Brown: The Last Discovery of America.* New York, NY: Viking Press, 2002.

Rowner, Ilai. *The Event: Theory and Literature.* Lincoln, NE: University of Nebraska Press, 2015.

Schaeffer, Jean-Marie. "Literary Studies and Literary Experience." Trans. Kathleen Antonioli. *New Literary History* 44: 2 (Spring 2013), 267–283.

Stavans, Ilán, Ed. et al. *The Norton Anthology of Latino Literature.* New York, NY: W. W. Norton, 2010.

Suárez, Lucía M. *The Tears of Hispaniola: Haitian and Dominican Diaspora Memory.* Gainesville: University Press of Florida, 2006.

Trouillot, Michel-Rolphe. *Silencing the Past: Power and the Production of History.* Boston, MA: Beacon Press, 1995.

Vargas, Jennifer Harford. *Forms of Dictatorship: Power, Narrative, and Authoritarianism in the Latina/o Novel.* Oxford: Oxford UP, 2018.

Viego, Antonio. *Dead Subjects: Toward a Politics of Loss in Latino Studies.* Durham, NC: Duke UP, 2007.

White, Hayden. *The Content of the Form: Narrative Discourse and Historical Representation.* Baltimore: Johns Hopkins UP, 1987.

Wiegman, Robyn. *Object Lessons.* Durham, NC: Duke UP, 2012.

INDEX

CPSIA information can be obtained
at www.ICGtesting.com
Printed in the USA
LVHW031841300919
632719LV00011B/156/P